HOW TO AVOID FEDERAL DRUG CONSPIRACY AND FIREARMS CHARGES

L. GREEN

HOW TO AVOID FEDERAL DRUG CONSPIRACY AND FIREARMS CHARGES

ISBN 9781449954178

Copyright © 2009 by L. GREEN

All rights reserved. No part of this book may be reproduced or transmitted in any form or by any means without written permission of the author.

Published by
Midnight Express Books
Helping inmates publish & sell books
POBox 69
Berryville AR 72616

Acknowledgement

I want to thank my lovely children De'Andre, Denise, A'Dashia, and Dominick for hanging in there with dear ol' Dad. My love goes to Ronete McGaughy for her support and friendship. To Floyd of Maxwell's New and Used for all his help and favors. My cousin Chris Bridges gave his valuable time to help me with this project. Valencia Smith and Keith Traylor pushed me to finish this book and without their help I would still be thinking about finishing it. My parents and my other family, I want to tell them I love them deeply.

Foreword

"He that has committed no crime by day,
fears not a knock on the door by night."

America has millions of people who either use or sell drugs; more than 2 million people have been either convicted of a felony or are waiting on a disposition of a felony case. The federal government alone houses close to 300,000 people. Most are in the Bureau of Prisons and the rest are in holding facilities with charges pending. A large percentage of federal arrests are drug and gun related.

How To Avoid a Federal Drug Conspiracy and Firearm Charges book gives readers complete insight on how indictments work for either gun or drug indictments.

Users and sellers of illegal drugs along with their friends and families learn how easily anyone can be indicted with a drug conspiracy. Friends and family members learn that supporting users and sellers might land them in jail for aiding and abetting.

This book will help you understand how prosecutors come up with a sentence length. You are able to calculate your own offense levels, criminal history points and use the sentencing table to find a sentence in months.

Convicted felons learn exactly what constructive possession is and the penalties that are waiting if convicted of firearm charges.

The entire process is discussed from arrest to being sent to the Bureau of Prisons.

Included in this book are a few important B.O.P. policies that readers might want to know. BOP prisons are listed with their locations and explanations of prison camp, FCI Low, FCI Medium and United States Penitentiary.

Anyone who reads this book will have the power to add up their custody and destination points to see which level prison they will possibly end up.

Within this book readers will be able to learn what it takes to avoid a federal drug conspiracy and firearm charges.

Table of Contents

Chapter 1 - CONSPIRACY 1

Chapter 2 - FIREARMS 7

Chapter 3 - YOU'VE BEEN ARRESTED 11

Chapter 4 - PUBLIC vs. PRIVATE ATTORNEY 15

Chapter 5 - PLEA AGREEMENTS 17

Chapter 6 - BUREAU OF PRISONS 21

CONCLUSION 25

Appendix 27

Chapter 1 - CONSPIRACY

Conspiracy is an agreement between two or more persons to commit a crime or accomplish a legal purpose through illegal action.

The federal conspiracy charge is nasty and practically unbeatable. Most defendants are not able to successfully fight the indictment without going to prison. No matter how much money you throw at it.

It does not take very much to find your name on a conspiracy. Here is an example of a conspiracy case. Howard worked every day and had no criminal background with only a few traffic tickets. He sold powder cocaine to a few people once a week. His long time friend, John, was his best customer. John worked at the local hospital along with his wife. Howard had no idea that John used meth with his wife on occasion. John sent his wife to buy some Meth during a lunch break. On her way back she was stopped by federal agents and arrested for possession of meth. She told agents everything, including her husband's involvement. John was arrested for Aiding and Abetting because he gave her the money to buy the drugs. The meth dealer was arrested for selling meth. John agreed to help himself and his wife by setting up Howard. Howard was arrested for selling powder cocaine. To make matters worse Howards friend, Donny, was at the house sometimes when John came by. Donny had no involvement in selling or using any illegal drugs. But since John told agents he was there and knew what was going on, agents arrested Donny as well. In turn Howard could not stand to go to jail, so he agreed to work for the federal agents. Between Howard and the meth dealer the people involved grew to more than 50 persons. Almost every person arrested by federal authorities agreed to cooperate in one way or another. When the indictments were finished there were 57 names listed on one indictment; all this happened over one arrest of a user. Most of the people on the indictment have no clue who some of the other people are on the indictment. Out of those 57 people on the indictment six were caught with drugs.

Conspiracy indictments can start years back; there is no statute of limitations on a federal conspiracy. That means even if a person stops selling or involving themselves with illegal drugs 3 years ago, they can still be indicted on federal drug conspiracy charges. All this can happen just on an informant's word. No drugs. No money. The problem is even if he or she lied, you will have to prove it. Unfortunately during trial it's his or her word against yours. Not to mention you probably are not going to take the stand in your own defense to prove that person is a liar. Your chances on winning are slim, but good luck if you're forced to go to trial.

If your only involvement with drugs was minimal, for example, 5 grams of cocaine for personal use, your indictment will still list all the drugs your other co-defendants had or sold. So don't be surprised to see 5 kilograms of crack cocaine plus or 10,000 ecstasy pills on your indictment even though you or anyone you personally knew never used or possessed these drugs; this is called 'Ghost Dope' – drugs that are not in evidence.

The federal government gets away with listing 50 plus people on one indictment because they are saying 'they had one common goal to use, sell, buy or transport illegal drugs' even though everyone doesn't know each other. Our federal prosecutors can charge you with no certain amount of drugs on the indictment also. Crazy laws our federal government has.

If you are involved with any illegal drugs, you are one arrest away from a federal indictment. You might be dealing with an informant right now. The feds could be watching you right now. How would you know? Informants/friends are responsible for populating federal and state prisons. But of course your friends and family are all tuff and would never rat on another.

Aiding and Abetting is a federal charge that you will see along with most drug conspiracy charges. Prosecutors are saying that you helped the conspirator do something illegal. It doesn't have to be much nor does it have to be a lot of times - just once.

Example: Cindy often took money and gifts her boyfriend brought her. She did not know how he received the items but accepted them anyway. She would rent cars and sometimes put property in her name because her credit was pretty good.

One day police came and arrested her boyfriend for selling drugs. Cindy was spared from arrest at that moment. Her boyfriend refused to cooperate. The feds quickly changed his mind and did as they asked. They had threatened to arrest innocent Cindy for Aiding and Abetting. This example happens very often. Not every person is lucky like Cindy. Most are arrested and forced to cooperate at least with a statement. Federal prosecutors are very zealous and will arrest anyone they believe helped drug dealers and broke federal law. Yes, that means grandparents, mom and dad. No matter how small the help was.

Men, please stop involving our women, friends and family, in our illegal business. Not all women can stand up to the pressure of federal prosecutors threats. Not to mention being away from their children. Try to remember this, the next time you tell her to hold something or give her money you made from selling drugs. She cannot put money on your books or accept collect phone calls if she is in a cell next door to you. Then you wonder why she stopped talking to you and received a bond.

In short, any person that receives, relieves, comforts, or assists the felon in any manner and helps the felon to escape arrest or punishment. Even if you're not a part of the conspiracy, you can still be put on a federal drug indictment as an accessory to the conspirator. It will not matter if happens before or after the actual felony act.

If you fall into this category, stop helping or else you'll need to read chapter 3.

Last but not least for the people who live abroad or travel abroad, you have not been forgotten. Do not think this government will not snatch you off a beach and take you to federal court in Miami and say they found you on South Beach when they arrested you; better think again. It is true that some countries will not extradite, but don't hold your breath. You never know what extremes this government will go to, to bring you before the court. You cannot send anything illegal to the United States through another person, either on purpose or accident, and think you're going to get away with it. If that person who got caught with the drugs tells your name, you will have a federal drug conspiracy waiting on you. If possible, federal agents and your government probably will try to find you and arrest you.

Knowledge is the Key to Prevention.

Chapter 2 - FIREARMS

This is not the wild, wild West. If you have a felony and get caught with a gun, seen with a gun, use a gun, or are near a gun, you probably will find yourself in jail. How long? It depends on your criminal history, the weapon, and the events that are involved in your case.

Body armor, ammunition, cartridge cases, primer, bullets or propellant powder designed for use in any firearm is not allowed by felons.

It is true that some states allow felons to possess rifles and shotguns for hunting purposes. Check your state laws before you decide to drive down the street with that hunting rifle. The Feds have said they will only step in if situations warrant.

Not knowing the gun was there or saying it's not mine nor is it my property, will not stop federal prosecutors from charging you. Here is an example of a gun case.

City police serve a search warrant looking for a person with a state warrant. There are several people inside the house including children. The person that police are searching for is not there nor is the owner of the house. During the search police find one handgun under the couch where four men were found playing X-Box. Two of the men on the couch were convicted felons. No one inside the house admitted to knowing the gun was inside the house. The two men with felonies were indicted later for possession by a felon and the two men without felonies were charged with concealed weapon charges from state prosecutors. How can four people be charged with possessing one weapon that was not in their actual possession?

Here is another weapons case. Mark was a convicted felon but was off any probation or parole for 10 years. He was married and worked every day. He had no brushes with the law. He and his wife got into a verbal dispute one evening and his daughter-in-law calls the police. The couple lets the police inside the home and tries to explain that they were just arguing. Police run a warrant check and finds out Mark has a record. Police ask if there are any weapons inside the home and the daughter tells them that there is a gun in the closet. Police find the gun and it's registered to Marks wife. She bought the gun before the couple got married.

Police leave without arresting anyone. But two months later federal agents arrest Mark for possession of a firearm by a felon.

You're wondering how can this happen and why? It's called constructive possession. I'll explain. In the first case, what the federal prosecutors will try to prove is that the men knew that the weapon was there. The feds will say that all four men had power and intention to exercise dominion and control over the weapon. Confusing? If the prosecutors can prove you knew that gun was under the couch, they can prove you had access to it and therefore had control over it as well. If that is proved, then prosecutors can do that to a house full of people.

In the second case, Mark will have to prove that he did not know that his wife had a gun in the closet. Not good if everybody knows what's in the house and you do not. Mark is probably going to jail. But more than mere control and dominion over a place where a gun is found is required to establish constructive possession. That means that you have to know that the gun is there before you can be convicted of possessing it. You might have to prove it in trial.

There are dozens of scenarios that deal with constructive possession. I hope this gives you a perspective on the federal charge as per Sentencing Guidelines for 922(g)(1) and 924(e). In the Appendix pages 51-54 has guidelines for gun charges. Here are the mandatory minimums:

- The penalty for felon weapon possession is not less than 5 years.
- If you brandish the weapon, not less than 7 years.
- If the gun is discharged, not less than 10 years.
- If a sawed off or assault rifle, not less than 10 years.
- If a machine gun or you have a silencer/muffler, not less than 30 years.
- If you have a prior federal 924 charge and this is your 2nd time being charged, not less than 25 years: having a prior 924 charge and having a machine gun or silencer/muffler......Life! You have been warned!

"The cautious seldom err."
Confucius

Chapter 3 - YOU'VE BEEN ARRESTED

You've been arrested and indicted. What's next?

Well you didn't read chapters one and two. If you did, I hope your reading the next chapters for general knowledge.

I'm sure the federal agents are crawling all over your property and taking everything you own if it had anything to do with your crime. I know you're hoping that your people are being left alone because you mistakenly involved them in your business. You are on your way to your initial court hearing. The judge will read off your charges and the amount of time you're facing. The US Marshals will fingerprint and photograph you for their system. The judge will set another court date for you to receive a bond and lawyer. This usually happens in the first week after your arrest.

Every federal court district is different when it comes to giving a person a bond or probation. It's called probation because you have to report to him or her like you were on probation. Not many people receive a bond. They are pretty strict on who they allow to have one. One thing for sure, your record has to be almost clean. If you're lucky to get one, the judge could set your bond for let's say $50,000. The judge might just let you go on a signature or require you to put up 10%. Unless the court can prove your rich, you will receive a public defender.

One more thing to note about receiving a bond, the prosecutors will have a lot of say in either direction.

While you're sitting trying to figure out what happened. Keep your mouth shut. Bragging or discussing your case will get you in deeper trouble. Most of the people in there with you will use your words and testify on you for a 5K1/time cut. You have enough problems to deal with in your own indictment.

Speaking of that, you will receive a copy of your indictment and your charges along with a hopefully not long list of names in your indictment if it's a drug conspiracy. In most cases for gun charges, only your name will be in the indictment unless others are charged possessing the same weapon; the list of names are in order of importance. I mean that if your name is on the top of the list, then you're the leader, or at least that's what people are saying.

If there any names blacked out on your indictment that means that person is an informant, probably your homeboy or girl. If you have not received your copy of the indictment, it's probably sealed. Everybody in the indictment may have not been arrested yet; Feds don't want you to warn them.

Your problems haven't started yet. Learning how to use the guidelines can be stressful. In the Appendix pages 28 - 55, you're able to add your criminal history points, find your drug and drug amount charged in your indictment and use those with the sentencing table to find an offense level and sentence length. For weapons charges, in the Appendix page 51 you are able to do the same and learn what Armed Career Criminal is. The feds use felonies and misdemeanors to add to your criminal history. Yes, some traffic tickets you received will count against you.

Enhancements add levels to your offense. At this point, you will not know if you have any. To generalize, right now whether it's a gun or drug charge you are facing between 5 years and a life sentence. All federal felonies have a statutory mandatory minimal and a maximum range of time. Most drug cases fall in between 5 to 40 years, 10 years to life, 20 years to life and a mandatory life sentence; guns 5 years to life.

I'm going to explain how to understand what an offense level is and how enhancements work against you.

First thing you need to know every federal offense has a base level offense between 1 to 43, one being the lesser and 43 being the severest level. Let's use drugs as our example. Your indictment is charging you with 2 Kilos of powder cocaine. I would look in the Appendix page 30 for drug quantity guidelines and find 2 Kilos of cocaine. It says a level 28 as a base offense level. Then I can look how to add up my criminal history points, remembering that misdemeanors count. Now I can look at the sentencing table and find my offense level and criminal history category. Let's use category 6(VI). It says 140 to 175 months. That would be your guideline.

Enhancements play a part with the guidelines by raising both your offense level and mandatory minimums. Let's use the previous example of 2 Kilos at a base level of 28.

That level can be enhanced by what the feds call a leadership role for example. Leadership role means that you lead 5 or more persons in the conspiracy. That is a 4 point level increase.

28 + 4 = 32. 32 is your new offense level. The definitions of enhancements according to your role in the offense are also in the Appendix on page 57. When it comes to mandatory minimums, 2 Kilos would normally be between 5 years minimum and 40 years maximum. If you have a least 1 prior felony charge for either violence or drugs, the prosecutors will enhance that 5 to 40 to a minimum of 10 years to a maximum of life. Your guideline of 140 to 175 months would not change.

There are so many enhancements I could not include them all. Armed Career Criminal and Career Criminal are similar in their base level offense. Check in the Appendix pages 53-56 for full explanations of both. If your instant offense of conviction is a felony, a crime of violence or a controlled substance offense and the defendant has at least two prior felony convictions or either a crime of violence or a controlled substance offense, you are a Career Offender.

Simple gun possession is not a crime of violence according to the guidelines rules.

Here is some good news. You may receive a 3 point reduction off your base offense level for acceptance of responsibility for your offense and providing complete information to the government concerning your own involvement in the offense. Instead of a level 32 it would be a level 29. If you fight them, they will fight not to give you the 3 point reduction. I'm not saying you should not fight, make sure you know the rules to the game before you engage the enemy.

Chapter 4 - PUBLIC vs. PRIVATE ATTORNEY

*"He who asks, is a fool for five minutes.
But he who does not, is a fool forever."*

There are good and bad points in both situations. The stories can get ugly. I believe that if you have the money to spare, hire an attorney. If you're rich and the court knows it, you'll have to pay for one anyway. A lot of people wish they had not paid for a lawyer and still went to jail for 10 years. No one expects to pay a lawyer $20,000 and still have to face that amount of time. The question always remains, if you had a public defender, would you still receive the same amount of time? The guidelines speak for themselves. I guess since the judge doesn't have to follow the guidelines exactly, that a good lawyer could possibly get you less time than recommended.

The federal court system is designed to punish you according to your instant offense and past criminal history. The guidelines are supposed to give the court an idea of how many months he or she should sentence you. Your lawyer's job is to make sure your rights are preserved and honored. Your job is to make sure they do exactly that. When you plead guilty in federal court, you cannot take it back. "No! I change my mind" will not work; you give up all appeals. There is an exception if you can prove your lawyer failed to defend you properly. That is a 2255 motion for ineffective assistance from counsel; after you have been sentenced that is your only defense from sorry lawyers.

What can a private attorney provide for you? Will he or she make promises they cannot keep? In most cases they will tell you that they need a retainer to look over your case. How much? $500, $5,000, $10,000 or more? After all is said and done, you will still receive the exact amount of time that your guidelines recommend; what did you pay your attorney for? I do not know the answer. But it is sometimes a hard choice, especially if money is tight.

No matter who you decide to choose to defend you, this next discussion is very important.

Your Pre-Sentence Investigation Report (PSI). This report goes directly to the judge before you are sentenced and after you plead guilty. It will have your entire criminal history, your life, and anything that has to do with your indictment. The PSI might have errors in it that will affect your recommended sentence and sentencing. The judge usually will adhere to its findings as closely as possible. Make sure that you go over this report carefully. Only you know if there are any errors about your past and current case. It's your job to find errors and your attorney's job to correct them in court. Learn what's going on in your case by picking up a law book and asking questions.

Chapter 5 - PLEA AGREEMENTS

*"Reading without thinking will confuse you.
Thinking without reading will place you in danger."*

No matter what your indictment is, you must understand what you just plead guilty to. It's not just a piece of paper, it's your life. The feds will take it all away because you didn't read the agreement. As of now all federal inmates will do 85% of the total months he or she were sentenced to.

120 months x 85% = 8 years 5 months.

If you receive a fine, you will pay it in prison.

Discuss with your lawyer the amount of time you're facing with any possible enhancements well before you sign the plea. If you're able to lock an offense level in using rule 11(c) (1) (c) plea, do so. It would be your only possible protection against enhancements by the prosecutor. The judge still has the authority to overrule any pleas.

When you sign most plea agreements it is called an 'Open Plea'. This means that if you're facing a 10-to-life sentence the judge can sentence you anywhere in between 10-to-life. If you do get sentenced unfairly, in your opinion, you will have to appeal the sentence. The other bad thing about open pleas is you don't know what enhancements, if you have any, will be in the PSI report. You can sign a plea for 7 years and if you don't lock that in, your PSI could come out with 14 years because of enhancements.

After you sign a plea you will go to court to plead guilty for whatever you agreed to in the plea agreement. Are you sure of the charges you plead to? The PSI officer will come and interview you. They ask questions to make sure their information is correct. Now is the time to see what charges they are doing a report on. Ask! Do not make silly or irresponsible statements to this officer. A friend of mine cussed a PSI officer out and the judge sentenced him to 20 years and sent him to a USP. His PSI recommended only 10 years. He had no criminal history at all. So watch your mouth.

The B.O.P. has a 500 hour drug program where you can receive 18 months off your projected release date. That includes a 6 month halfway house. You must have drugs and alcohol in your PSI. Even though the judge recommends the drug program, the BOP will not allow you time off if you do not qualify.

If you have a gun case, only the 9th Circuit (west coast), is allowing the time off with gun charges. The director of the BOP says gun cases will be labeled as violent. This is why it is very important that you know what you plead guilty to. Even though you did not plead guilty to possessing a gun, the PSI officer will still enhance you because an informant said he or she saw you with a weapon.

For all those who are not aware it is not double jeopardy for the city, state and federal government to charge you with the same charges, or to use your prior convictions against you over and over again. Sorry, blame it on the Supreme Court.

Knowing a few BOP policies before you sign the plea will help you and your lawyer make good decisions. Agreeing to plead guilty to something you did not do or wasn't apart of might not get you more time, but might stop you from going to the prison camp for example.

Chapter 6 - BUREAU OF PRISONS

After all the waiting and fighting with the prosecutors, you have been sentenced. If you were allowed a bond/probation then most likely the court will allow you to turn yourself in wherever the BOP designates you. If you are in a holding facility, you will be transported to a Federal Transfer Center (FTC) to be processed. Your paperwork has been sent to the BOP already and you have been designated to a Prison. Your family can check with www.bop.com to find out where if you're not told in the transfer center. In the Appendix pages 72, 73 and 74 you can add up your custody and designation points to get an idea where you might be going. You will not be able to transfer with anything that is on your property or person. Cloths and other belongings must be mailed home or someone can pick them up; this includes legal work, too. Your money will follow you if you had some on your account. If you are arrested with money and transferred to a federal transfer center then back to a holding facility, like a county jail, your money will stay in the BOP until you return. It will not follow you back to a county jail.

BOP policy is to try to send you within a 500 mile radius of your home address from your PSI, not your indictment location. Radius is not driving miles. Radius is a 500 mile circle around your home address. To transfer you will need 18 months of good conduct. I have to make this perfectly clear. The BOP does not have to do what the sentencing judge recommends. The judge can recommend you go to a camp. Well the BOP might feel different and send you to a USP.

Prison camps are exactly what they sound like, CAMP. NO fence, one or two officers, and a whole lot of freedom to screw up. You must have 10 years or less and other things are considered before you are allowed to go there; for women the rules are different.

FCI Lows have two fences. Most inmates have less than 20 years. Not a lot of violence. Relaxed. Most people here are close to going home or a camp.

FCI Mediums are fenced in also. But it's night and day from a low to a medium. First thing you need to be aware is that it's a good chance that you will need that PSI to stay on the compound. Your PSI will say whether you cooperated with the Feds. According to the BOP they tried to stop this from happening.

They tried to make everyone get rid of theirs if they had it, but it didn't work. If you don't come up with yours, you will have to go 'Up Top' the hole or check-in. You will stay there until you receive it or be transferred elsewhere. If you think you can 'Buck' the inmate system, you might not 'Buck' anything else. Unlike the lows, the mediums operate in 'Cars'. This means that you should eat, hang out with, and support the inmates from your home city or state; this is for gang members, too. Cars are to regulate themselves, so respect levels are maintained. All cars have spoke persons. Any problems that come up can be resolved so a war won't break out and people die.

USPs are much like the mediums except for the large wall that surrounds them. Inmates can go from a USP to a Camp as long as they do not have a life sentence.

Goodtime is 54 days a year for each year that you're incarcerated; that's about 85%. You will have a projected goodtime release date based on good behavior; this does not include halfway house which has been moved up to 12 months.

You can lose good time by receiving a incident report or shot. Once you earn good time, it can never be taken away; once you lose it, it won't be restored without the director's ok. If you have a fight and lose 27 goodtime days, your release date will be moved back 27 days.

If you have a fine, you will pay it or you will not be able to get a job paying more than $28, plus you will not be able to buy food or clothing items at the store.

Your case manager will ask you to pay $25 every 3 months to pay your fine; $100 assessment is not a fine.

E-mail is not everywhere but its 5¢ a minute to read and send mail; no pictures or attachments.

You will have to attend G.E.D. classes if you do not have one and until you get it, you are only able to make $28 on any job you have.

You may spend $290 a month.

You get 300 minutes on the phone per month; you may call collect or pre-pay the phone call off your account. When you call, there is a prerecorded message that tells who you're calling that they are getting a phone call from a prison inmate and to accept the call, they only have to press 5.

UNICORE is privately owned company. People with fines are preferred and can get a job with them faster than those prisoners without fines. Once employed, half of your check will go towards your fine. People without fines are put on a long list and have to wait for an opening.

Your case manager is responsible for all your transfers; better hope you get a good one.

The BOP prisons offer a lot of training; it's free. Convicted felons need all the help they can get.

I wish you the best and hopefully you're reading this book before you get yourself into any trouble.

CONCLUSION

In conclusion, I hope that after reading this book people will change their actions about illegal drugs and gun involvement.

Federal Prosecutors are asking for too much time for convictions of our unlawful actions. And, for some reason, the people we elect to be our leaders think that harsher laws will stop citizens from breaking the law. NOT! More laws are more laws to be broken and more criminals to make; which in turn, is job security for law enforcement and anyone who makes money from law enforcement.

How many people would be out of work if there was no crime? Now that the Feds are hammering CEO's, Senators, and child molesters, there is talk about reform - mostly overcrowding and budget cuts for prisons.

Recently, though, law makers passed a crack bill reducing the offense level for some people convicted who received 'unfair' crack sentences; this law allowed some time to be taken off their sentence. Not everyone who had a crack cocaine case was affected though. The courts used their "discretion" to decide who will get the reduction and who will not. It was total 'B.S.' Yes, there was some relief, but it was still unfair.

Currently, a person gets more time when convicted for crack than they do for cocaine. But now, there is discussion to make crack and cocaine the same. We will see how that proposed change in the law will affect already sentenced inmates.

Crack has taken a back seat since the prevalence of Meth and "White America" is now feeling what crack dealers and users have always experienced with the Federal government - long prison terms.

Much reform is needed in Federal courts. They give out sentences with too much time for non-violent cases; where the state might give probation, the Feds give 10 years.

Another change is certainly needed regarding Federal Judges. Appointing them to a life time seat is stupid and irresponsible. They can violate our constitutional rights without penalty. You cannot sue them for it. If they were elected officials like other government heads, I think they would be more careful with what they do.

In the end, probably nothing will be done because there is just too much to re-do and there is too many overpaid, lazy government employees who only care about their own pockets.

On that note, if you are looking for a good job and have a pretty clean criminal record, I suggest that you try getting a job with the Bureau of Prisons; $25 hr and in the union. You don't even work very much – just open doors and tell inmates what to do.

Well, I'll end this note by repeating what our new president keeps telling us Americans - 'Time for Change.'

APPENDIX

Pages 28 – 55 cited from The Guidelines Manual

Pages 56 – 88 cited from the BOP Program Statement

PART D - OFFENSES INVOLVING DRUGS

1. UNLAWFUL MANUFACTURING, IMPORTING, EXPORTING, TRAFFICKING, OR POSSESSION; CONTINUING CRIMINAL ENTERPRISE

§2D1.1. Unlawful Manufacturing, Importing, Exporting, or Trafficking (Including Possession with Intent to Commit These Offenses); Attempt or Conspiracy

  (a) Base Offense Level (Apply the greatest):

    (1) 43, if the defendant is convicted under 21 U.S.C. § 841(b)(1)(A), (b)(1)(B), or (b)(1)(C), or 21 U.S.C. § 960(6)(1), (b)(2), or (b)(3), and the offense of conviction establishes that death or serious bodily injury resulted from the use of the substance and that the defendant committed the offense after one or more prior convictions for a similar offense; or

    (2) 38, if the defendant is convicted under 21 U.S.C. § 841(b) (1) (A), (b) (1) (B), or (b) (1) (C), or 21 U.S.C. § 960(b) (1), (b) (2), or (b) (3), and the offense of conviction establishes that death or serious bodily injury resulted from the use of the substance; or

    (3) The offense level specified in the Drug Quantity Table set forth in subsection (c) below.

  (b) Specific Offense Characteristics

    (1) If a dangerous weapon (including a firearm) was possessed, increase by 2 levels.

    (2) If the defendant unlawfully imported or exported a controlled substance under circumstances in which (A) an aircraft other than a regularly scheduled commercial air carrier was used to import or export

HOW TO AVOID FEDERAL DRUG CONSPIRACY AND FIREARMS CHARGES

the controlled substance, or (B) the defendant acted as a pilot, copilot, captain, navigator, flight officer, or any other operation officer aboard any craft or vessel carrying a controlled substance, increase by 2 levels. If the resulting offense level is less than level 26, increase to level 26.

(c) Drug Quantity Table is set forth on the following pages.

(d) Cross Reference

(1) If a victim was killed under circumstances that would constitute murder under 18 U.S.C. § 1111 had such killing taken place within the territorial or maritime jurisdiction of the United States, apply §2A1.1 First Degree Murder).

(c) DRUG QUANTITY TABLE

Base Offense Level   Controlled Substances and Quantity*

(1)   LEVEL 38

- 30 KG or more of Heroin (or the equivalent amount of other Schedule I or II Opiates);

- 150 KG or more of Cocaine (or the equivalent amount of other Schedule I or II Stimulants);

- 1.5 KG or more of Cocaine Base;

- 30 KG or more of PCP, or 3 KG or more of PCP (actual);

- 30 KG or more of Methamphetamine, or 3 KG or more of Methamphetamine (actual), or 3 KG or more of "Ice";

- 300 G or more of LSD (or the equivalent amount of other Schedule I or II Hallucinogens);

- 12 KG or more of Fentanyl;

- 3 KG or more of a Fentanyl Analogue;

- 30,000 KG or more of Marihuana;

- 6,000 KG or more of Hashish;

- 600 KG or more of Hashish Oil.

Base Offense Level   Controlled Substances and Quantity*

(2) LEVEL 36

- At least 10 KG but less than 30 KG of Heroin (or the equivalent amount of other Schedule I or II Opiates);

- At least 50 KG but less than 150 KG of Cocaine (or the equivalent amount of other Schedule I or II Stimulants);

- At least 500 G but less than 1.5 KG of Cocaine Base;

- At least 10 KG but less than 30 KG of PCP, or at least 1 KG but less than 3 KG of PCP (actual);

- At least 10 KG but less than 30 KG of Methamphetamine, or at least 1 KG but less than 3 KG of Methamphetamine (actual), or at least 1 KG but less than 3 KG of "Ice;

- At least 100 G but less than 300 G of LSD (or the equivalent amount of other Schedule I or II Hallucinogens);

- At least 4 KG but less than 12 KG of Fentanyl;

- At least 1 KG but less than 3 KG of a Fentanyl Analogue;

- At least 10,000 KG but less than 30,000 KG of Marihuana;

- At least 2,000 KG but less than 6,000 KG of Hashish;

- At least 200 KG but less than 600 KG of Hashish Oil.

Base Offense Level   Controlled Substances and Quantity*

(3) LEVEL 34

- At least 3 KG but less than 10 KG of Heroin (or the equivalent amount of other Schedule I or II Opiates);

- At least 15 KG but less than 50 KG of Cocaine (or the equivalent amount of other Schedule I or II Stimulants);

- At least 150 G but less than 500 G of Cocaine Base;

- At least 3 KG but less than 10 KG of PCP, or at least 300 G but less than 1 KG of PCP (actual);

- At least 3 KG but less than 10 KG of Methamphetamine, or at least 300 G but less than 1 KG of Methamphetamine (actual), or at least 300 G but less than 1 KG of "Ice";

- At least 30 G but less than 100 G of LSD (or the equivalent amount of other Schedule I or II Hallucinogens);

- At least 1.2 KG but less than 4 KG of Fentanyl;

- At least 300 G but less than 1 KG of a Fentanyl Analogue;

- At least 3,000 KG but less than 10,000 KG of Marihuana;

- At least 600 KG but less than 2,000 KG of Hashish;

- At least 60 KG but less than 200 KG of Hashish Oil.

Base Offense Level   Controlled Substances and Quantity*

(4) LEVEL 32

- At least 1 KG but less than 3 KG of Heroin (or the equivalent amount of other Schedule I or II Opiates);

- At least 5 KG but less than 15 KG of Cocaine (or the equivalent amount of other Schedule I or II Stimulants);

- At least 50 G but less than 150 G of Cocaine Base;

- At least 1 KG but less than 3 KG of PCP, or at least 100 G but less than 300 G of PCP (actual);

- At least 1 KG but less than 3 KG of Methamphetamine, or at least 100 G but less than 300 G of Methamphetamine (actual), or at least 100 G but less than 300 G of "Ice";

- At least 10 G but less than 30 G of LSD (or the equivalent amount of other Schedule I or II Hallucinogens);

- At least 400 G but less than 1.2 KG of Fentanyl;

- At least 100 G but less than 300 G of a Fentanyl Analogue;

- At least 1,000 KG but less than 3,000 KG of Marihuana;

- At least 200 KG but less than 600 KG of Hashish;

- At least 20 KG but less than 60 KG of Hashish Oil.

Base Offense Level   Controlled Substances and Quantity*

(5) LEVEL 30

- At least 700 G but less than 1 KG of Heroin (or the equivalent amount of other Schedule I or H Opiates);

- At least 3.5 KG but less than 5 KG of Cocaine (or the equivalent amount of other Schedule I or II Stimulants);

- At least 35 G but less than 50 G of Cocaine Base;

- At least 700 G but less than 1 KG of PCP, or at least 70 G but less than 100 0-of PCP (actual);

- At least 700 G but less than 1 KG of Methamphetamine, or at least 70 G but less than 100 G of Methamphetamine (actual), or at least 70 G but less than 100 G of "Ice";

- At least 7 G but less than 10 G of LSD (or the equivalent amount of other Schedule I or II Hallucinogens);

- At least 280 G but less than 400 G of Fentanyl;

- At least 70 G but less than 100 G of a Fentanyl Analogue;

- At least 700 KG but less than 1,000 KG of Marihuana;

- At least 140 KG but less than 200 KG of Hashish;

- At least 14 KG but less than 20 KG of Hashish Oil.

Base Offense Level   Controlled Substances and Quantity*

(6) LEVEL 28

- At least 400 G but less than 700 G of Heroin (or the equivalent amount of other Schedule I or II Opiates);

- At least 2 KG but less than 3.5 KG of Cocaine (or the equivalent amount of other Schedule I or II Stimulants);

- At least 20 G but less than 35 G of Cocaine Base;

- At least 400 G but less than 700 G of PCP, or at least 40 G but less than 70 G of PCP (actual);

- At least 400 G but less than 700 G of Methamphetamine, or at least 40 G but less than 70 G of Methamphetamine (actual), or at least 40 G but less than 70 G of "Ice";

- At least 4 G but less than 7 G of LSD (or the equivalent amount of other Schedule I or II Hallucinogens);

- At least 160 G but less than 280 G of Fentanyl;

- At least 40 G but less than 70 G of a Fentanyl Analogue;

- At least 400 KG but less than 700 KG of Marihuana;

- At least 80 KG but less than 140 KG of Hashish;

- At least 8 KG but less than 14 KG of Hashish Oil.

Base Offense Level   Controlled Substances and Quantity*

(7) LEVEL 26

- At least 100 G but less than 400 G of Heroin (or the equivalent amount of other Schedule I or II Opiates);

- At least 500 G but less than 2 KG of Cocaine (or the equivalent amount of other Schedule I or II Stimulants);

- At least 5 G but less than 20 G of Cocaine Base;

- At least 100 G but less than 400 G of PCP, or at least 10 G but less than 40 G of PCP (actual);

- At least 100 G but less than 400 G of Methamphetamine, or at least 10 G but less than 40 G of Methamphetamine (actual), or at least 10 G but less than 40 G of "Ice";

- At least 1 G but less than 4 G of LSD (or the equivalent amount of other Schedule

- I or II Hallucinogens);

- At least 40 G but less than 160 G of Fentanyl;

- At least 10 G but less than 40 G of a Fentanyl Analogue;

- At least 100 KG but less than 400 KG of Marihuana;

- At least 20 KG but less than 80 KG of Hashish;

HOW TO AVOID FEDERAL DRUG CONSPIRACY AND FIREARMS CHARGES

Base Offense Level   Controlled Substances and Quantity*

(8) LEVEL 24

- At least 80 G but less than 100 G of Heroin (or the equivalent amount of other Schedule I or II Opiates);

- At least 400 G but less than 500 G of Cocaine (or the equivalent amount of other Schedule I or II Stimulants);

- At least 4 G but less than 5 G of Cocaine Base;

- At least 80 G but less than 100 G of PCP, or at least 8 G but less than 10 G of PCP (actual);

- At least 80 G but less than 100 G of Methamphetamine, or at least 8 G but less than 10 G of Methamphetamine (actual), or at least 8 G but less than 10 G of "Ice";

- At least 800 MG but less than 1 G of LSD (or the equivalent amount of other Schedule I or H Hallucinogens);

- At least 32 G but less than 40 G of Fentanyl;

- At least 8 G but less than 10 G of a Fentanyl Analogue;

- At least 80 KG but less than 100 KG of Marihuana;

- At least 16 KG but less than 20 KG of Hashish;

- At least 1.6 KG but less than 2 KG of Hashish Oil.

Base Offense Level   Controlled Substances and Quantity*

(9) LEVEL 22

- At least 60 G but less than 80 G of Heroin (or the equivalent amount of other Schedule I or II Opiates);

- At least 300 G but less than 400 G of Cocaine (or the equivalent amount of other Schedule I or H Stimulants);

- At least 3 G but less than 4 G of Cocaine Base;

- At least 60 G but less than 80 G of PCP, or at least 6 G but less than 8 G of PCP (actual);

- At least 60 G but less than 80 G of Methamphetamine, or at least 6 G but less than 8 G of Methamphetamine (actual), or at least 6 G but less than 8 G of "Ice";

- At least 600 MG but less than 800 MG of LSD (or the equivalent amount of other Schedule I or H Hallucinogens);

- At least 24 G but less than 32 G of Fentanyl;

- At least 6 G but less than 8 G of a Fentanyl Analogue;

- At least 60 KG but less than 80 KG of Marihuana;

- At least 12 KG but less than 16 KG of Hashish;

- At least 1.2 KG but less than 1.6 KG of Hashish Oil.

Base Offense Level   Controlled Substances and Quantity*

(10)   LEVEL 20

- At least 40 G but less than 60 G of Heroin (or the equivalent amount of other Schedule I or H Opiates);

- At least 200 G but less than 300 G of Cocaine (or the equivalent amount of other Schedule I or II Stimulants);

- At least 2 G but less than 3 G of Cocaine Base;

- At least 40 G but less than 60 G of PCP, or at least 4 G but less than 6 G of PCP (actual);

- At least 40 G but less than 60 G of Methamphetamine, or at least 4 G but less than 6 G of Methamphetamine (actual), or at least 4 G but less than 6 G of "Ice";

- At least 400 MG but less than 600 MG of LSD (or the equivalent amount of other Schedule I or II Hallucinogens);

- At least 16 G but less than 24 G of Fentanyl;

- At least 4 G but less than 6 G of a Fentanyl Analogue;

- At least 40 KG but less than 60 KG of Marihuana;

- At least 8 KG but less than 12 KG of Hashish;

- At least 800 G but less than 1.2 KG of Hashish Oil;

- 20 KG or more of Secobarbital (or the equivalent amount of other Schedule I or II Depressants) or Schedule III substances (except Anabolic Steroids);

- 40,000 or more units of Anabolic Steroids.

Base Offense Level   **Controlled Substances and Quantity***

(11) LEVEL 18

- At least 20 G but less than 40 G of Heroin (or the equivalent amount of other Schedule I or II Opiates);

- At least 100 G but less than 200 G of Cocaine (or the equivalent amount of other Schedule I or II Stimulants);

- At least 1 G but less than 2 G of Cocaine Base;

- At least 20 G but less than 40 G of PCP, or at least 2 G but less than 4 G of PCP (actual);

- At least 20 G but less than 40 G of Methamphetamine, or at least 2 G but less than 4 G of Methamphetamine (actual), or at least 2 G but less than 4 G of "Ice";

- At least 200 MG but less than 400 MG of LSD (or the equivalent amount of other Schedule I or II Hallucinogens);

- At least 8 G but less than 16 G of Fentanyl;

- At least 2 G but less than 4 G of a Fentanyl Analogue;

- At least 20 KG but less than 40 KG of Marihuana;

- At least 5 KG but less than 8 KG of Hashish;

- At least 500 G but less than 800 G of Hashish Oil;

- At least 10 KG but less than 20 KG of Secobarbital (or the equivalent amount of other Schedule I or II Depressants) or Schedule HI substances (except Anabolic Steroids);

- At least 20,000 but less than 40,000 units of Anabolic Steroids.

Base Offense Level   Controlled Substances and Quantity*

(12) LEVEL 16

- At least 10 G but less than 20 G of Heroin (or the equivalent amount of other Schedule I or II Opiates);

- At least 50 G but less than 100 G of Cocaine (or the equivalent amount of other Schedule I or II Stimulants);

- At least 500 MG but less than 1 G of Cocaine Base;

- At least 10 G but less than 20 G of PCP, or at least 1 G but less than 2 G of PCP (actual);

- At least 10 G but less than 20 G of Methamphetamine, or at least 1 G but less than 2 G of Methamphetamine (actual), or at least 1 G but less than 2 G of "Ice";

- At least 100 MG but less than 200 MG of LSD (or the equivalent amount of other Schedule I or II Hallucinogens);

- At least 4 G but less than 8 G of Fentanyl;

- At least 1 G but less than 2 G of a Fentanyl Analogue;

- At least 10 KG but less than 20 KG of Marihuana;

- At least 2 KG but less than 5 KG of Hashish;

- At least 200 G but less than 500 G of Hashish Oil;

- At least 5 KG but less than 10 KG of Secobarbital (or the equivalent amount of other Schedule I or II Depressants) or Schedule III substances (except Anabolic Steroids);

- At least 10,000 but less than 20,000 units of Anabolic Steroids.

Base Offense Level   Controlled Substances and Quantity*

(13) LEVEL 14

- At least 5 G but less than 10 G of Heroin (or the equivalent amount of other Schedule I or II Opiates);

- At least 25 G but less than 50 G of Cocaine (or the equivalent amount of other Schedule I or II Stimulants);

- At least 250 MG but less than 500 MG of Cocaine Base;

- At least 5 G but less than 10 G of PCP, or at least 500 MG but less than 1 G of PCP (actual);

- At least 5 G but less than 10 G of Methamphetamine, or at least 500 MG but less than 1 G of Methamphetamine (actual), or at least 500 MG but less than 1 G of "Ice";

- At least 50 MG but less than 100 MG of LSD (or the equivalent amount of other Schedule I or H Hallucinogens);

- At least 2 G but less than 4 G of Fentanyl;

- At least 500 MG but less than 1 G of a Fentanyl Analogue;

- At least 5 KG but less than 10 KG of Marihuana;

- At least 1 KG but less than 2 KG of Hashish;

- At least 100 G but less than 200 G of Hashish Oil;

- At least 2.5 KG but less than 5 KG of Secobarbital (or the equivalent amount of other Schedule I or II Depressants) or Schedule Ill substances (except Anabolic Steroids);

- At least 5,000 but less than 10,000 units of Anabolic Steroids.

Base Offense Level   Controlled Substances and Quantity*

(14) LEVEL 12

- Less than 5 G of Heroin (or the equivalent amount of other Schedule I or II Opiates);

- Less than 25 G of Cocaine (or the equivalent amount of other Schedule I or II Stimulants);

- Less than 250 MG of Cocaine Base;

- Less than 5 G of PCP, or less than 500 MG of PCP (actual);

- Less than 5 G of Methamphetamine, or less than 500 MG of Methamphetamine (actual), or less than 500 MG of "Ice";

- Less than 50 MG of LSD (or the equivalent amount of other Schedule I or II Hallucinogens);

- Less than 2 G of Fentanyl;

- Less than 500 MG of a Fentanyl Analogue;

- At least 2.5 KG but less than 5 KG of Marihuana;

- At least 500 G but less than 1 KG of Hashish;

- At least 50 G but less than 100 G of Hashish Oil;

- At least 1.25 KG but less than 2.5 KG of Secobarbital (or the equivalent amount of other Schedule I or II Depressants) or Schedule III substances (except Anabolic Steroids);

- At least 2,500 but less than 5,000 units of Anabolic Steroids;

- 20 KG or more of Schedule IV substances.

Base Offense Level   Controlled Substances and Quantity*

(15) LEVEL 10

- At least 1 KG but less than 2.5 KG of Marihuana;

- At least 200 G but less than 500 G of Hashish;

- At least 20 G but less than 50 G of Hashish Oil;

- At least 500 G but less than 1.25 KG of Secobarbital (or the equivalent amount of other Schedule I or II Depressants) or Schedule III substances (except Anabolic Steroids);

- At least 1,000 but less than 2,500 units of Anabolic Steroids;

- At least 8 KG but less than 20 KG of Schedule IV substances.

HOW TO AVOID FEDERAL DRUG CONSPIRACY AND FIREARMS CHARGES

Base Offense Level   Controlled Substances and Quantity*

(16) LEVEL 8

- At least 250 G but less than 1 KG of Marihuana;

- At least 50 G but less than 200 G of Hashish;

- At least 5 G but less than 20 G of Hashish Oil;

- At least 125 G but less than 500 G of Secobarbital (or the equivalent amount of other Schedule I or II Depressants) or Schedule III substances (except Anaholic Steroids);

- At least 250 but less than 1,000 units of Anabolic Steroids;

- At least 2 KG but less than 8 KG of Schedule IV substances;

- 20 KG or more of Schedule V substances.

Base Offense Level   Controlled Substances and Quantity*

(17) LEVEL 6

- Less than 250 G of Marihuana;

- Less than 50 G of H4shish;

- Less than 5 G of Hashish Oil;

- Less than 125 G of Secobarbital (or the equivalent amount of other Schedule I or

- II Depressants) or Schedule III substances (except Anaholic Steroids);

- Less than 250 units of Anabolic Steroids;

- Less than 2 KG of Schedule IV substances;

- Less than 20 KG of Schedule V substances.

---

*Unless otherwise specified, the weight of a controlled substance set forth in the table refers to the entire weight of any mixture or substance containing a detectable amount of the controlled substance.

HOW TO AVOID FEDERAL DRUG CONSPIRACY AND FIREARMS CHARGES

Effective November 1 2007, the United States Sentencing Commission lines were amended as follows:

2D1 1(C)

(1) Level 38   4.5 KG or more of cocaine base

(2) Level 36   More than 1.5KG but less than 4.5KG of cocaine base

(3) Level 34   At least 500G but less than 1.5KG of cocaine base

(4) Level 32   At least 150G but less than 500G of cocaine base

(5) Level 30   At least 50G but less than 150G of cocaine base

(6) Level 28   At least 35G but less than 503 cocaine base

(7) Level 26   At least 20G but less than 33G of cocaine base

(8) Level 24   At least 5G but less than 20G of cocaine base

(9) Level 22   At least 43 but less than 5G of cocaine base

(10) Level 20   At least 3G but less than 4G of cocaine base

(11) Level 18   At least 23 but less than 3G of cocaine base

(12) Level 16   At least 1G but less than 2G of cocaine base

(13) Level 14   At least 500MG but less than 1G of cocaine base

(14) Level 12   Less than 500MG of cocaine base

SENTENCING TABLE
(in months of imprisonment)

	Offense Level	Criminal History Category (Criminal History Points)					
		I (0 or 1)	II (2 or 3)	III (4, 5, 6)	IV (7, 8, 9)	V (10, 11, 12)	VI (13 or more)
Zone A	1	0 - 6	0 - 6	0 - 6	0 - 6	0 - 6	0 - 6
	2	0 - 6	0 - 6	0 - 6	0 - 6	0 - 6	1 - 7
	3	0 - 6	0 - 6	0 - 6	0 - 6	2 - 8	3 - 9
	4	0 - 6	0 - 6	0 - 6	2 - 8	4 - 10	6 - 12
	5	0 - 6	0 - 6	1 - 7	4 - 10	6 - 12	9 - 15
	6	0 - 6	1 - 7	2 - 8	6 - 12	9 - 15	12 - 18
Zone B	7	0 - 6	2 - 8	4 - 10	8 - 14	12 - 18	15 - 21
	8	0 - 6	4 - 10	6 - 12	10 - 16	15 - 21	18 - 24
	9	4 - 10	6 - 12	8 - 14	12 - 18	18 - 24	21 - 27
	10	6 - 12	8 - 14	10 - 16	15 - 21	21 - 27	24 - 30
Zone C	11	8 - 14	10 - 16	12 - 18	18 - 24	24 - 30	27 - 33
	12	10 - 16	12 - 18	15 - 21	21 - 27	27 - 33	30 - 37
Zone D	13	12 - 18	15 - 21	18 - 24	24 - 30	30 - 37	33 - 41
	14	15 - 21	18 - 24	21 - 27	27 - 33	33 - 41	37 - 46
	15	18 - 24	21 - 27	24 - 30	30 - 37	37 - 46	41 - 51
	16	21 - 27	24 - 30	27 - 33	33 - 41	41 - 51	46 - 57
	17	24 - 30	27 - 33	30 - 37	37 - 46	46 - 57	51 - 63
	18	27 - 33	30 - 37	33 - 41	41 - 51	51 - 63	57 - 71
	19	30 - 37	33 - 41	37 - 46	46 - 57	57 - 71	63 - 78
	20	33 - 41	37 - 46	41 - 51	51 - 63	63 - 78	70 - 87
	21	37 - 46	41 - 51	46 - 57	57 - 71	70 - 87	77 - 96
	22	41 - 51	46 - 57	51 - 63	63 - 78	77 - 96	84 - 105
	23	46 - 57	51 - 63	57 - 71	70 - 87	84 - 105	92 - 115
	24	51 - 63	57 - 71	63 - 78	77 - 96	92 - 115	100 - 125
	25	57 - 71	63 - 78	70 - 87	84 - 105	100 - 125	110 - 137
	26	63 - 78	70 - 87	78 - 97	92 - 115	110 - 137	120 - 150
	27	70 - 87	78 - 97	87 - 108	100 - 125	120 - 150	130 - 162
	28	78 - 97	87 - 108	97 - 121	110 - 137	130 - 162	140 - 175
	29	87 - 108	97 - 121	108 - 135	121 - 151	140 - 175	151 - 188
	30	97 - 121	108 - 135	121 - 151	135 - 168	151 - 188	168 - 210
	31	108 - 135	121 - 151	135 - 168	151 - 188	168 - 210	188 - 235
	32	121 - 151	135 - 168	151 - 188	168 - 210	188 - 235	210 - 262
	33	135 - 168	151 - 188	168 - 210	188 - 235	210 - 262	235 - 293
	34	151 - 188	168 - 210	188 - 235	210 - 262	235 - 293	262 - 327
	35	168 - 210	188 - 235	210 - 262	235 - 293	262 - 327	292 - 365
	36	188 - 235	210 - 262	235 - 293	262 - 327	292 - 365	324 - 405
	37	210 - 262	235 - 293	262 - 327	292 - 365	324 - 405	360 - life
	38	235 - 293	262 - 327	292 - 365	324 - 405	360 - life	360 - life
	39	262 - 327	292 - 365	324 - 405	360 - life	360 - life	360 - life
	40	292 - 365	324 - 405	360 - life	360 - life	360 - life	360 - life
	41	324 - 405	360 - life	360 - life	360 - life	360 - life	360 - life
	42	360 - life	360 - life	360 - life	360 - life	360 - life	360 - life
	43	life	life	life	life	life	life

November 1, 1994

Sentencing Table

HOW TO AVOID FEDERAL DRUG CONSPIRACY AND FIREARMS CHARGES

Worksheet C (Criminal History)

Defendant _____ Docket Number _____

Date Defendant Commenced Participation in Instant Offense (Earliest Date of Relevant Conduct) _____

1. **3 Points** for each prior ADULT sentence of imprisonment exceeding ONE YEAR and ONE MONTH imposed within 15 YEARS of the defendant's commencement of the instant offense OR resulting in incarceration during any part of that 15-YEAR period. (See §§4A1.1(a) and 4A1.2.)

2. **2 Points** for each prior sentence of imprisonment of at least 60 DAYS resulting from an offense committed ON OR AFTER the defendant's 18th birthday not counted under §4A1.1(a) imposed within 10 YEARS of the instant offense; and

   2 Points for each prior sentence of imprisonment of at least 60 DAYS resulting from an offense committed BEFORE the defendant's 18th birthday not counted under §4A1.1(a) from which the defendant was released from confinement within 5 YEARS of the instant offense. (See §§4A1.1(b) and 4A1.2.)

3. **1 Point** for each prior sentence resulting from an offense committed ON OR AFTER the defendant's 18th birthday not counted under §4A1.1(a) or §4A1.1(b) imposed within 10 YEARS of the instant offense; and

   1 Point for each prior sentence resulting from an offense committed BEFORE the defendant's 18th birthday not counted under §4A1.1(a) or §4A1.1(b) imposed within 5 YEARS of the instant offense. (See §§4A1.1(c) and 4A1.2.)

   NOTE: A maximum of **4 Points** may be imposed for the prior sentences in Item 3.

Date of Imposition	Offense	Sentence	Release Date**	Guideline Section	Criminal History Pts.

* Indicate with an asterisk those offenses where defendant was sentenced as a juvenile

** A release date is required in only three instances:

   a. When a sentence covered under §4A1.1(a) was imposed more than 15 years prior to the commencement of the instant offense but release from incarceration occurred within such 15-year period;

   b. When a sentence counted under §4A1.1(b) was imposed for an offense committed prior to age 18 and more than 5 years prior to the commencement of the instant offense, but release from incarceration occurred within such 5-year period; and

   c. When §4A1.1(e) applies because the defendant was released from custody on a sentence counted under 4A1.1(a) or 4A1.1(b) within 2 years of the instant offense or was still in custody at the time of the instant offense (see Item 5).

Total Criminal History Points for §§4A1.1(a), 4A1.1(b), and 4A1.1(c) (Items 1,2,3) ☐

Rev. 10/94

WORK SHEET C (Criminal History) page 1

Worksheet C
Page 2

Defendant _____ Docket Number _____

4. **2 Points** if the defendant committed the instant offense while under any criminal justice sentence (e.g., probation, parole, supervised release, imprisonment, work release, escape status). (See §§4A1.1(d) and 4A1.2.) List the type of control and identify the sentence from which control resulted. Otherwise, enter 0 Points.

5. **2 Points** if the defendant committed the instant offense less than 2 YEARS after release from imprisonment on a sentence counted under §4A1.1(a) or (b) or while in imprisonment or escape status on such a sentence. However, enter only 1 Point for this item if 2 points were added at Item 4 under §4A1.1(d). (See §§4A1.1(e) and 4A1.2.) List the date of release and identify the sentence from which release resulted. Otherwise, enter 0 Points.

6. **1 Point** for each prior sentence resulting from a conviction of a crime of violence that did not receive any points under §4A1.1(a), (b), or (c) because such sentence was considered related to another sentence resulting from a conviction of a crime of violence. *Provided*, that this item does not apply where the sentences are considered related because the offenses occurred on the same occasion. (See §§4A1.1(f) and 4A1.2.) Identify the crimes of violence and briefly explain why the cases are considered related. Otherwise, enter 0 Points.

Note: A maximum of 3 Points may be imposed for Item 6.

_____
_____
_____
_____
_____
_____
_____

7. **Total Criminal History Points** (Sum of Items 1-6)

8. **Criminal History Category** (Enter here and on Worksheet D, Item 4)

Total Points	Criminal History Category
0-1	I
2-3	II
4-6	III
7-9	IV
10-12	V
13 or more	VI

Rev. 10/94

WORK SHEET C (Criminal History) page 2

FIREARMS

§2K2.1. Unlawful Receipt, Possession, or Transportation of Firearms or Ammunition; Prohibited Transactions Involving Firearms or Ammunition

   (a)   Base Offense Level (Apply the Greatest):

   (1) 26, if the defendant had at least two prior felony convictions of either a crime of violence or a controlled substance offense, and the instant offense involved a firearm listed in 26 U.S.C. § 5845(a); or

   (2) 24, if the defendant had at least two prior felony convictions of either a crime of violence or a controlled substance offense; or

   (3) 22, if the defendant had one prior felony conviction of either a crime of violence or a controlled substance offense, and the instant offense involved a firearm listed in 26 U.S.C. § 5845(a); or

   (4) 20, if the defendant had one prior felony conviction of either a crime of violence or a controlled substance offense; or is a prohibited person, and the offense involved a firearm listed in 26 U.S.C. § 5845(a); or

   (5) 18, if the offense involved a firearm listed in 26 U.S.C. § 5845(a); or

   (6) 14, if the defendant is a prohibited person; or

   (7) 12, except as provided below; or

(8) 6, if the defendant is convicted under 18 U.S.C. § 922(c), (e), (f), or (m).

    (b)   Specific Offense Characteristics

1. If the offense involved three or more firearms, increase as follows:

# of Firearms	Increase in Level
(A) 3-4	add 1
(B) 5-7	add 2
(C) 8-12	add 3
(D) 13-24	add 4
(E) 25-49	add 5
(F) 50 or more	add 6

(2) If the defendant, other than a defendant subject to subsection (a)(1), (a)(2), (a)(3), (a)(4), or (a)(5), possessed all ammunition and firearms solely for lawful sporting purposes or collection, and did not unlawfully discharge or otherwise unlawfully use such firearms or ammunition, decrease the offense level determined above to level 6.

(3) If the offense involved a destructive device, increase by 2 levels.

(4) If any firearm was stolen, or had an altered or obliterated serial number, increase by 2 levels.

Provided, that the cumulative offense level determined above shall not exceed level 29.

(5) If the defendant used or possessed any firearm or ammunition in connection with another felony offense; or possessed or transferred any firearm or ammunition with knowledge, intent, or reason to be-

HOW TO AVOID FEDERAL DRUG CONSPIRACY AND FIREARMS CHARGES

lieve that it would be used or possessed in connection with another felony offense, increase by 4 levels. If the resulting offense level is less than level 18, increase to level 18.

§4B1.4. Armed Career Criminal

    a) A defendant who is subject to an enhanced sentence under the provisions of 18 U.S.C. § 924(e) is an armed career criminal.

    b) The offense level for an armed career criminal is the greatest of:

        (1) The offense level applicable from Chapters Two and Three; or

        (2) The offense level from §4B1.1 (Career Offender) if applicable; or

        (1)   (A) 34, if the defendant used or possessed the firearm or ammunition in connection with a crime of violence or controlled substance offense, as defined in §4B1.2(1), or if the firearm possessed by the defendant was of a type described in 26 U.S.C. § 5845(a)*; or

            (B) 33, otherwise.*

*If an adjustment from §3E1.1 (Acceptance of Responsibility) applies, decrease the offense level by the number of levels corresponding to that adjustment.

    c) The criminal history category for an armed career criminal is the greatest of:

(1) The criminal history category from Chapter Four, Part A (Criminal History), or §4B1.1 (Career Offender) if applicable; or

(2) Category VI, if the defendant used or possessed the firearm or ammunition in connection with a crime of violence or controlled substance offense, as defined in §4B1.2(1), or if the firearm possessed by the defendant was of a type described in 26 U.S.C. § 5845(a); or

(3) Category IV.

Commentary

Application Note:

1. This guideline applies in the case of a defendant subject to an enhanced sentence under 18 U.S.C. § 924(e). Under 18 U.S.C. § 924(e) (1), a defendant is subject to an enhanced sentence if the instant offense of conviction is a violation of 18 U.S.C. § 922(g) and the defendant has at least three prior convictions for a "violent felony" or "serious drug offense," or both, committed on occasions different from one another. The terms "violent felony" and "serious drug offense" are defined in 18 U.S.C. § 924(e) (2). It is to be noted that the definitions of "violent felony" and "serious drug offense" in 18 U.S.C. § 924(e)(2) are not identical to the definitions of "crime of violence" and "controlled substance offense" used in §4B1.1 (Career Offender), nor are the time periods for the counting of prior sentences under §4A1.2 (Definitions and Instructions for Computing Criminal History) applicable to the determination of whether a defendant is subject to an enhanced sentence under 18 U.S.C. § 924(e).

PART B-CAREER OFFENDERS & CRIMINAL LIVELIHOOD

§4MA. Career Offender

A defendant is a career offender if (1) the defendant was at least eighteen years old at the time of the instant offense, (2) the instant offense of conviction is a felony that is either a crime of violence or a controlled substance offense, and (3) the defendant has at least two prior felony convictions of either a crime of violence or a controlled substance offense. If the offense level for a career criminal from the table below is greater than the offense level otherwise applicable, the offense level from the table below shall apply. A career offender's criminal history category in every case shall be Category VI.

	Offense Statutory Maximum	Offense Level*
A.	Life	37
B.	25 years or more	34
C.	20 years or more, but less than 25 years	32
D.	15 years or more, but less than 20 years	29
E.	10 years or more, but less than 15 years	24
F.	5 years or more, but less than 10 years	17
G.	More than 1 year, but less than 5 years	12

*If an adjustment from §3E1.1 (Acceptance of Responsibility) applies, decrease the offense level by the number of levels corresponding to that adjustment.

Commentary

Application Notes:

1. "Crime of violence," "controlled substance offense," and "two prior felony convictions" are defined in §4B1.2.
2. "Offense Statutory Maximum," for the purposes of this guideline, refers to the maximum term of imprisonment authorized for the offense of conviction that is a crime of violence or controlled substance offense, not including any increase in that maximum term under a sentencing enhancement provision that applies because of the defendant's prior criminal record (such sentencing enhancement provisions are contained, for example, in 21 U.S.C. § 841(b)(1)(A), (b)(1)(B), (b)(1)(C), and (b)(1)(D)). For example, where the statutory maximum term of imprisonment under 21 U.S.C. § 841(b)(1)(C) is increased from twenty years to thirty years because the defendant has one or more qualifying prior drug convictions, the "Offense Statutory Maximum" for the purposes of this guideline is twenty years and not thirty years. If more than one count of conviction is of a crime of violence or controlled substance offense, use the maximum authorized term of imprisonment for the count that authorizes the greatest maximum term of imprisonment.

HOW TO AVOID FEDERAL DRUG CONSPIRACY AND FIREARMS CHARGES

PART B - ROLE IN THE OFFENSE

Introductory Commentary

This Part provides adjustments to the offense level based upon the role the defendant played in committing the offense. The determination of a defendant's role in the offense is to be made on the basis of all conduct within the scope of §1B1.3 (Relevant Conduct), i.e., all conduct included under §1B1.3 (a) (1)-(4), and not solely on the basis of elements and acts cited in the count of conviction.

When an offense is committed by more than one participant, §3B1.1 or §3B1.2 (or neither) may apply. Section 3B1.3 may apply to offenses committed by any number of participants.

Historical Note: Effective November 1, 1987. Amended effective November 1, 1990 (see Appendix C, amendment 345); November 1, 1992 (see Appendix C, amendment 456).

§3B1.1. Aggravating Role

Based on the defendant's role in the offense, increase the offense level as follows:

> (a) If the defendant was an organizer or leader of a criminal activity that involved five or more participants or was otherwise extensive, increase by 4 levels.
>
> (b) If the defendant was a manager or supervisor (but not an organizer or leader) and the criminal activity involved five or more participants or was otherwise extensive, increase by 3 levels.
>
> (c) If the defendant was an organizer, leader, manager, or supervisor in any criminal activity other than described in (a) or (b), increase by 2 levels.

DEFINITION OF ROLES INVOLVED IN DRUG OFFENSES

To determine whether an individual involved with a drug offense rose to the level of an organizer or leader, read the "Offense Conduct" section of the Presentence Investigation Report, and any other available information (i.e., Statement of Reasons, U.S. Attorney Report, etc.) to determine what the individual's role was in the criminal activity. The role definitions below are grouped into two categories: Those that rise to the level of organizer/leader; and, those that do not.

ORGANIZER/LEADER

Importer/High-Level Supplier: imports or otherwise supplies large quantities of drugs; is at or near the top of the distribution chain; has ownership interest in drugs (not merely transporting drugs for another individual); usually supplies drugs to other drug distributors and does not deal in retail amounts; may employ no or very few subordinates.

Organizer/Leader: Organizes leads, directs, or otherwise runs a drug distribution organization. Receives the largest share of the profits and has the greatest decision-making authority.

Grower/Manufacturer: grows, cultivates, or manufactures a controlled substance, and is the principal owner of the drugs. (Keep in mind, the intent of this definition is to capture the individual who has the capability to manufacture enormous amounts of drugs in his garage/lab for example, and not the individual who is growing only five marijuana plants in his basement.)

Financier/Money Launderer: provides money for purchase, importation, manufacture, cultivation, transportation, or distribution of drugs; launders proceeds of drug sales or purchases.

Aircraft Pilot/Vessel Captain: pilots vessel or aircraft; requires special skill; does not include inmate who is the only participant directing a small boat (i.e., a speed boat) onto which drugs had been loaded from a "mother ship" (such person is a courier).

NOT A DRUG ORGANIZER/LEADER

Manager: serves as a lieutenant to assist one of the above; manages all or a significant portion of the manufacturing, importation, or distribution operation; takes instructions from one of the above and conveys to subordinates; directly supervises at least one other co-participant in an organization of at least five co-participants.

Bodyguard/Strongman/Debt Collector: provides physical and personal security for another co-participant in the offense; collects debts owed, or punishes recalcitrant persons.

Chemists/Cooks/Chemical Supplier: produces LSD, methamphetamine, crack cocaine, or other illegal drugs, but does not qualify as a Grower/Manufacturer because he/she is not the principal owner of the drugs. Chemical supplier does not handle drugs themselves but engages in the unlawful diversion, sale, or furnishing of listed chemicals or equipment used in the synthesis or manufacturing of controlled substances.

Supervisor: supervises at least one other co-participant, however, has limited authority and does not qualify as a Manager.

Street-Level Dealer: distributes retail quantities directly to the user.

Broker/Steerer/Go-Between: arranges for two parties to buy/sell drugs, or directs potential buyer to a potential seller.

Courier: transports or carries drugs with the assistance of a vehicle or other equipment. Includes situations where individual, who is otherwise considered to be a crew member, is the only participant directing a vessel (e.g., a speed boat) onto which drugs had been loaded from a "mother ship".

Mule: transports or carries drugs internally or on their person, often by airplane, or by walking across a border. Also includes an individual who only transports or carries drugs in baggage, souvenirs, clothing, or otherwise.

Renter/Storer: provides (for profit/compensation) own residence, structures (barns, storage bins, buildings), land, or equipment for use to further the offense. This inmate is distinguished from the enabler because he/she is paid (in some way) for his/her services.

Money runner: transports/carries money and/or drugs to and from the street-level dealer.

Off-loader/Loader: performs the physical labor required to put large quantities of drugs into storage, hiding, or onto some mode of transportation.

Gopher/Lookout/Deckhand/Worker/Employee: performs very limited, low-level function in the offense (whether or not ongoing); includes running errands, answering the telephone, receiving packages, packaging the drugs, manual labor, acting as lookout to provide early warnings during meetings, exchanges, or offloading, or acting as deckhand/crew member on vessel or aircraft used to transport large quantities of drugs.

Enabler (Passive): plays no more than a passive role in the offense, knowingly permitting a certain unlawful criminal activity to take place without actually being involved with the activity; may be coerced or unduly influenced to play such a function (e.g., a parent or grandparent threatened with displacement from a home unless they permit the activity to take place), or may do so as "a favor" (without compensation).

User Only: possessed small amount of drugs apparently for personal use only; no apparent function in any conspiratorial criminal activity.

Wholesaler: sells more than retail/user-level quantities (greater than one ounce) in a single transaction.

HOW TO AVOID FEDERAL DRUG CONSPIRACY AND FIREARMS CHARGES

SECURITY DESIGNATION DATA

The Security Designation Data section (beginning with Item 9) of the Inmate Load and Security Designation form (BP-337) records sentencing, programing recommendations, and background information from the Judgment, the Statement of Reasons (SOR),and the PSR. This information is used to determine the inmate's security level.

The documentation used to assess the Criminal History Points must be provided as specified in all cases.

9. **HISTORY OF VIOLENCE**

9. HISTORY OF VIOLENCE		NONE	>15 YEARS	10-15 YEARS	5-10 YEARS	<5 YEARS	
	MINOR	0	1	1	3	5	
	SERIOUS	0	2	4	6	7	

Enter the appropriate number of points that reflect any history of violence, considering only those acts for which there are documented findings of guilt (i.e., DHO, Court, Parole, Mandatory Release, or Supervised Release Violation). This item includes the individual's entire background of criminal violence, excluding the current term of confinement.

Exception: Any institution disciplinary hearing (UDC or DHO) finding that a prohibited act was committed during the current term of confinement will be scored as a history item. DSCC staff must review the Chronological Disciplinary Record (CDR) for inmates who were previously housed in a federal institution or contract facility. Any violent act(s) reflected on the CDR must be scored as a history item. State disciplinary findings must be scored unless there is documentation that the state disciplinary proceedings did not afford due process protection to the inmate.

Severity of violence is determined by the offense behavior regardless of the conviction/finding of guilt offense. History of Violence points combine both seriousness and recency of prior violent incidents to assess the propensity for future violence. Therefore, if there is more than one incident of violence, score the combination of seriousness and recency that yields the highest point score. Prior periods of incarceration will be considered a "history" item if the inmate was physically released from custody and then returned to serve either a violation or a new sentence. In determining time frames, use the date of the documented behavior. Documented information from a juvenile, Youth Corrections Act (YCA) or District of Columbia Youth Rehabilitation Act (DCYRA) adjudication can be used unless the record has been expunged or vacated.

Minor History of Violence - Aggressive or intimidating behavior which is not likely to cause serious bodily harm or death (e.g., simple assault, fights, domestic disputes, etc.) There must be a finding of guilt.

Serious History of Violence - Aggressive or intimidating behavior which is likely to cause serious bodily harm or death (e.g., aggravated assault, domestic violence, intimidation involving a weapon, incidents involving arson or explosives, rape, etc.). There must be a finding of guilt.

Example: If an offender was found guilty of homicide 20 years ago and a simple assault 3 years ago, assign 5 points for the simple assault. Or in another case, the offender had guilty findings for homicide 12 years ago; aggravated assault 8 years ago; and fighting 2 years ago, score 6 points for the aggravated assault 8 years ago.

NOTE: Attempted suicide, self-mutilation and possession of weapons are not applicable behaviors for History of Violence scoring. In addition, verbal threats (such as Code 203- Threatening Bodily Harm) are to be viewed as minor violence.

10. **HISTORY OF ESCAPE OR ATTEMPTS**

10. HISTORY OF ESCAPE OR ATTEMPTS		NONE	>15 YEARS	10-15 YEARS	5-10 YEARS	<5 YEARS	
	MINOR	0	1	1	2	3	
	SERIOUS	0	3(S)	3(S)	3(S)	3(S)	

Enter the appropriate number of points that reflect the escape history of the individual considering only those acts for which there are documented findings of guilt (i.e., DHO, Court, Parole, Mandatory Release, or Supervised Release Violation). Escape history includes the individual's entire background of escapes or attempts to escape from confinement, or absconding from community supervision, excluding the current term of confinement.

Exception: Any institution disciplinary hearing (UDC or DHO) finding that a prohibited act was committed during the current term of confinement will be scored as a history item. DSCC staff must review the Chronological Disciplinary Record (CDR) for inmates who were previously housed in a federal institution or contract facility. Any escape(s) or attempt(s) reflected on the CDR must be scored as a history item. State disciplinary findings are to be scored unless there is documentation that the state disciplinary proceedings did not afford due process protection to the inmate.

Fleeing or Eluding Arrest, Failure to Appear for traffic violations, Absconding, runaways from foster homes and similar

HOW TO AVOID FEDERAL DRUG CONSPIRACY AND FIREARMS CHARGES

behavior should not to be scored under the Escape History item, even if clearly documented, but should be considered on a case-by-case basis under the Management Variable "Greater Security." Failure to Appear or Flight to Avoid Prosecution for any offense however, must be counted when there is a documented finding of guilt.

In determining time frames, use the date of the documented occurrence. Documented information from a juvenile, YCA, or DCYRA adjudication can be used unless the record has been expunged or vacated.

Minor History of Escape - An escape from an open institution or program (e.g., minimum security facility, CCC, furlough) not involving any actual or threat of violence. Also includes military AWOL, Bail Reform Act, Flight to Avoid Prosecution, and Absconding from Community Supervision. There must be a finding of guilt except as previously noted.

Serious History of Escape - An escape from secure custody with or without threat of violence. Also includes escapes from an open facility or program with actual threat of violence. There must be a finding of guilt. S = 3 points and requires application of PSF L.

11. **TYPE OF DETAINER**

11. TYPE OF DETAINER	0 = NONE	3 = MODERATE	7 = GREATEST
	1 = LOWEST/LOW MODERATE	5 = HIGH	

Enter the appropriate number of points that reflect detainer status. Refer to the Offense Severity Scale, Appendix A. Determination is based on the offense of the most serious detainer.

- If there is a pending charge, points based on the documented behavior are assigned on the "Type of Detainer" item. If the pending charges or detainer involve a probation violation, use the most severe documented behavior in the original offense as the basis for assigning points in scoring the detainer.

  If law enforcement officials indicate a firm intent to lodge a detainer, consider it lodged. Score a concurrent state sentence as a detainer only if it is expected that the state sentence will exceed the federal sentence. However, score consecutive state sentences, lodged state detainers, and/or state parole violation terms/warrants as detainers.

- Consecutive federal sentences are ordinarily not lodged as detainers because federal sentences are computed as they are received. If there is more than one sentence, the most severe offense will be used as "Severity of Current Offense."

    Example: For an individual with two detainers for Violation of Firearms Act (Moderate severity level) and one for Extortion (High severity level), use High = 5 points and enter "5".

- No points will be awarded for U.S. Parole Commission warrants (adjudicated or unadjudicated). However, the original offense behavior will be factored into the criminal history points and the violation behavior (including new offense behavior) will be scored as the instant offense.

- No points will be awarded for ICE detainers. However, each case will be carefully reviewed to determine whether the PSF for Deportable Alien is applicable.

12. **AGE**

12. AGE	0 = 55 and over	4 = 25 through 35	
	2 = 36 through 54	8 = 24 or less	

SENTRY will automatically enter the appropriate number of points based on the inmate's date of birth. Staff do not have to manually enter an offender's age or points on the BP-337. If the offenders date of birth is unknown, SENTRY will default to a score of 4 points.

13. **EDUCATION LEVEL**

13. EDUCATION LEVEL	0 = Verified High School Degree or GED 1 = Enrolled in and making satisfactory progress in GED Program 2 = No verified High School Degree/GED and not participating in GED Program	
13a. HIGHEST GRADE COMPLETED		

Enter the appropriate number of points that reflect the inmate's verified education level at the time of designation.

In addition to the points assigned for the education level, the highest grade completed (HGC) will also be recorded on the BP-337. For example, an inmate who began, but did not complete the 7th grade will be given a 6 in the HGC field. Similarly, a GED will be given a 12, a college graduate a 16, a Master's degree an 18, and a Ph.D. a 21 (the maximum allowed) in the HGC field. The value entered for the HGC should, unless missing, be consistent with the points assessed for the inmates education level. If missing, enter a "U" for unknown.

14. **DRUG/ALCOHOL ABUSE**

| 14. DRUG/ALCOHOL ABUSE | 0 - Never/ >5 Years | 1 = <5 Years | |

Enter the appropriate number of points that reflect drug or alcohol abuse by the inmate. Examples of drug or alcohol abuse include: a conviction of a drug or alcohol related offense, a parole or probation violation based on drug or alcohol abuse, positive drug test, a DUI, detoxification, etc. Absent any information similar to the above, an inmate's self-report is sufficient to score this item. If this information is unknown enter a "U" and the item will be scored as zero.

15. **SECURITY POINT TOTAL**

| 15. SECURITY POINT TOTAL | |

Enter the sum of Items 5 through 14.

16. **PUBLIC SAFETY FACTORS**

| 16. PUBLIC SAFETY FACTORS | A-NONE
B-DISRUPTIVE GROUP (males only)
C-GREATEST SEVERITY OFFENSE (males only)
F-SEX OFFENDER
G-THREAT TO GOVERNMENT OFFICIALS
H-DEPORTABLE ALIEN | I-SENTENCE LENGTH (males only)
K-VIOLENT BEHAVIOR (females only)
L-SERIOUS ESCAPE
M-PRISON DISTURBANCE
N-JUVENILE VIOLENCE
O-SERIOUS TELEPHONE ABUSE | |

See Chapter 5, pages 7-13 for a description of Public Safety Factors and their application.

17. **REMARKS**

17. REMARKS

A brief explanation of the current offense(s) is required in the "Remarks" section. Similarly, Pre-Sentence Investigation Report information relevant to other scoring items that may have an impact on the designation process or the transportation of the inmate (e.g., medical or psychiatric information, or arrest behavior with no conviction) must also be noted in this section. Refer to Appendix C, Standard Abbreviations/Terms. Also, the

3. **DESIGNATOR.** The Designator will enter his or her initials.

4. **REASON FOR DESIGNATION.** Designators will use this section to document whether the primary reason for designation was for security reasons or for management reasons.

- Enter "S" if the inmate's security level is the primary reason for designation and the placement is within normal guidelines. If "S" is entered, SENTRY will not permit an entry in the "Management Reason" field.

- Enter "M" if a Management Variable is the primary reason for designation and placement is outside normal guidelines. When "M" is entered, you must enter the appropriate Management Variable(s) (e.g., B = Judicial Recommendation, D = Release Residence, etc.) under the Management Reason item. While one MGTV is generally sufficient, a maximum of three MGTVs may be entered into SENTRY. In the unlikely event that an inmate's designation facility is inconsistent with his or her MSL, at least one additional non-MSL MGTV must be added to support and explain the inconsistency.

- When it is necessary to place an inmate at a particular institution temporarily in order to receive a parole hearing, a secondary designation is required. The DSCC will notify the Warden of the secondary institution via GroupWise. Following the hearing, the institution where the inmate was first placed should review the secondary designation and contact the DSCC if the results of the hearing indicate that a change in the secondary designation is required.

5. **MANAGEMENT VARIABLES.** See Chapter 5, pages 1-6 for a description of Management Variables and their application.

6. **REMARKS.** The Designator will enter any relevant information not already recorded that may have an impact on the designation process or the transportation of the inmate.

HOW TO AVOID FEDERAL DRUG CONSPIRACY AND FIREARMS CHARGES

OFFENSE SEVERITY SCALE

GREATEST SEVERITY

Aircraft Piracy - placing plane or passengers in danger
Arson - substantial risk of death or bodily injury
Assault - serious bodily injury intended or permanent or life threatening bodily injury resulting)
Car Jacking - any
Drug Offense - see criteria below*
Escape - closed institution, secure custody, force or weapons used
Espionage - treason, sabotage, or related offenses
Explosives - risk of death or bodily injury
Extortion - weapon or threat of violence
Homicide or Voluntary Manslaughter - any
Kidnaping - abduction, unlawful restraint, demanding or receiving ransom money
Robbery - any
Sexual offenses - rape, sodomy, incest, carnal knowledge, transportation with coercion or force for commercial purposes
Toxic Substances/Chemicals: - weapon to endanger human life
Weapons - distribution of automatic weapons, exporting sophisticated weaponry, brandishing or threatening use of a weapon

* Any **drug offender** whose current offense includes the following criteria will be scored in the Greatest severity category:

The offender was part of an organizational network and he or she organized or maintained ownership interest/profits from **large-scale** drug activity,

AND

The drug amount equals or exceeds the amount below:

Cocaine - greater than or equal to 10,000 gm, 10 K, or 22 lb
Cocaine Base "Crack" - greater than or equal to 31 gm
Hashish - greater than or equal to 250,000 gm, 250 K, or 551 lb
Marijuana - greater than or equal to 620,000 gm, 620 K, or 1,367 lb
PCP - greater than or equal to 100,000 mg, 100 gm, or 20,000 dosage units
Heroin or Opiates - greater than or equal to 2,000 gm, 2 K, or 4.4 lb
Methamphetamine - greater than or equal to 16,000 gm, 17 K, or 35 lbs
Other illicit drugs: - Amphetamine, Barbiturates, LSD, etc. greater than or equal to 250,000 dosage units

HIGH SEVERITY
Arson - other
Cruelty to Children - any
Drugs (For Females only)
Cocaine - greater than or equal to 10,000 gm, 10 K, Or 22 lb
Cocaine Base "Crack" - greater than or equal to 31 gm
Hashish - greater than or equal to 250,000 gm, 250 K, Or 551 lb
Marijuana - greater than or equal to 620,000 gm, 620 K, Or 1,367 lb
PCP - greater than or equal to 100,000 mg, 100 gm, or 20,000 dosage units
Heroin or Opiates - greater than or equal to 2,000 gm, 2 K, or 4.4 lb
Methamphetamine - greater than or equal to 16,000 gm, 17 K, or 35 lb
Other illicit drugs - Amphetamine, Barbiturates, LSD etc. - greater than or equal to 250,000 dosage units
Explosives - other
Extortion - other
Involuntary manslaughter - includes vehicular homicide
Residential Burglary - with evidence that occupants were in dwelling during the commission of the offense
Rioting - any
Sexual Offenses - sexual exploitation of children, unlawful sexual conduct with a minor, pornography
Stalking - any
Threatening Communications - with conduct evidencing intent to carry out such threat
Toxic Substances/Chemicals - other

HOW TO AVOID FEDERAL DRUG CONSPIRACY AND FIREARMS CHARGES

MODERATE SEVERITY
Assault - other
Auto Theft - any
Breaking and Entering - any
Burglary - other
Child Abandonment - any
Contempt of Court - criminal contempt
Drugs Cocaine - greater than or equal to 400 gm, .4 K, or .88 lb
Cocaine Base "Crack" - greater than or equal to 1 gm
Hashish - greater than or equal to 11,000 gm, 11 K, or 24 lb
Marijuana - greater than or equal to 25,000 gm, 25 K, or 55 lb
PCP - greater than or equal to 4,000 mg, 4 gm, or .14 oz
Heroin or Opiates - greater than or equal to 80 gm, .08 K, or .18 lb
Methamphetamine - greater than or equal to 667 gm, .67 K, or 1.47 lb
Other illicit drugs - Amphetamine, Barbiturates, LSD, etc. greater than or equal to 10,000 dosage units, .05 K, or .11 lb
Escape - walkaway from open institution, failure to appear/bail reform act, no threat of violence involved
Immigration Offenses - transportation of unlawful aliens
Obstruction of Justice - any
Property Offenses - over $250,000, includes theft, fraud, tax evasion, forgery, currency offenses
Sexual Offenses - other
Weapons - other

LOW-MODERATE SEVERITY
Bigamy - Polygamy
Drugs Cocaine - less than 400 gm, .4 K, or .88 lb
Cocaine Base "Crack" - less than 1 gm
Hashish - less than 11,000 gm, 11 K, or 24 lb
Marijuana - less than 25,000 gm, 25 K, or 55 lb
PCP - less than 4,000 mg, 4 gm, or .14 oz
Heroin or Opiates - less than 80 gm, .08 K, or .18 lb
Methamphetamine - less than 667 gm, .67 K, or 1.47 lb
Other illicit drugs - Amphetamine, Barbiturates, LSD, etc., less than 10,000 dosage units, .05 K, or .11 lb
Indecent Exposure - indecent acts, lewd behavior
Immigration Offenses - other
Post-Release Supervision Violation - technical, administrative
Property Offenses - valued between $2,000 and $250,000)

LOWEST SEVERITY
Drugs - personal use
Gambling Law Violation - any
Liquor Law Violation - any
Property Offenses - less than $2,000
Suspicion - any
Traffic Laws - any
Vagrancy - any
Vandalism - any

MARIJUANA EQUIVALENT CHART	
DRUG	MARIJUANA EQUIVALENT
1 gm of Heroin	1000 gm
1 gm of Cocaine Powder	200 gm
1 gm of Methamphetamine	2000 gm
1 gm of LSD	100,000 gm
1 gm of "crack" cocaine	20,000 gm
1 gm of Hashish Oil	50 gm
For other drug equivalents, please refer to the U.S. Sentencing Commission Guidelines Manual.	

MEASUREMENT CONVERSION TABLE	
1 oz = 28.35 gm	1 gm = 1 ml (liquid)
1 lb = 453.6 gm	1 liter = 1,000 ml
1 lb = 0.4536 kg	1 kg = 1,000 gm
1 gal = 3.785 liters	1 gm = 1,000 mg
1 qt = 0.946 liters	1 grain = 64.8 mg

HOW TO AVOID FEDERAL DRUG CONSPIRACY AND FIREARMS CHARGES

```
BP-A337.051        INMATE LOAD AND SECURITY DESIGNATION  CDFRM
SEP 06
U.S. DEPARTMENT OF JUSTICE                    FEDERAL BUREAU OF PRISONS
```

INMATE LOAD DATA

1. REGISTER NUMBER:
2. LAST NAME   3. FIRST NAME   4. MIDDLE   5. SUFFIX
6. RACE   7. SEX   8. ETHNIC ORIGIN   9. DATE OF BIRTH
10. OFFENSE/SENTENCE
11. FBI NUMBER   12. SSN NUMBER
13. STATE OF BIRTH   14. OR COUNTRY OF BIRTH 15. CITIZENSHIP
16. ADDRESS-STREET
17. CITY   18. STATE   19. ZIP   20. OR FOREIGN COUNTRY
21. HEIGHT   FT   IN   22. WEIGHT   LBS   23. HAIR COLOR   24. EYE COLOR
25. ARS ASSIGNMENT:

SECURITY DESIGNATION DATA

1. JUDGE   2. REC FACILITY   3. REC PROGRAM   4. USM OFFICE
5. VOLUNTARY SURRENDER STATUS   0 = NO   (-3) = YES
   IF YES, MUST INDICATE: 5a. VOLUNTARY SURRENDER DATE:
                             5b. VOLUNTARY SURRENDER LOCATION:
6. MONTHS TO RELEASE :
7. SEVERITY OF   0 = LOWEST   3 = MODERATE   7 = GREATEST
   CURRENT OFFENSE   1 = LOW MODERATE   5 = HIGH
8. CRIMINAL HISTORY   0 = 0-1   4 = 4-6   8 = 10-12
   SCORE   2 = 2-3   6 = 7-9   10- 13 +
8a. SOURCE OF DOCUMENTED   - PRESENTENCE INVESTIGATION REPORT or   - NCIC III
9. HISTORY OF   NONE   >15 YEARS   10-15 YEARS   5-10 YEARS   <5 YEARS
   VIOLENCE   MINOR   0   1   1   3   5
              SERIOUS 0   2   4   6   7
10. HISTORY OF   NONE   >15 YEARS   >10 YEARS   5-10 YEARS   <5 YEARS
    ESCAPE OR MINOR   0   1   1   2   3
    ATTEMPTS   SERIOUS 0   3(S)   3(S)   3(S)   3(S)
11. TYPE OF   0 = NONE   3 = MODERATE   7 = GREATEST
    DETAINER   1 = LOWEST/LOW MODERATE 5 = HIGH
12. AGE   0 = 55 and over   4 = 25 through 35
                          2 = 36 through 54   8 = 24 or less
13. EDUCATION   0 = Verified High School Degree or GED
    LEVEL   1 = Enrolled in and making satisfactory progress in GED Program
                  2 = No verified High School Degree/GED and not participating in GED Program
13.a HIGHEST GRADE COMPLETED
14. DRUG/ALCOHOL ABUSE   0 = NEVER/>5 Years   1 = <5 Years
15. SECURITY POINT TOTAL   0
16. PUBLIC   A-NONE   I-SENTENCE LENGTH (males only)
    SAFETY   B-DISRUPTIVE GROUP (males only) K-VIOLENT BEHAVIOR (females only)
    FACTORS   C-GREATEST SEVERITY OFFENSE (males only) L-SERIOUS ESCAPE
              F-SEX OFFENDER   M-PRISON DISTURBANCE
              G-THREAT TO GOVERNMENT OFFICIALS N-JUVENILE VIOLENCE
              H-DEPORTABLE ALIEN   O-SERIOUS TELEPHONE ABUSE
17. REMARKS

18. OMDT REFERRAL (YES/NO)
(This form may be replicated via WP)   Replaces BP-S337 of FEB 02
```

*BP-337*
```

BP-A338.051	CUSTODY CLASSIFICATION CDFRM	
SEP 06 U.S. DEPARTMENT OF JUSTICE		FEDERAL BUREAU OF PRISONS

A. IDENTIFYING DATA

1. INSTITUTION CODE	2. UNIT	3. DATE
4. NAME		5. REGISTER NUMBER

6. MANAGEMENT VARIABLES	A - NONE B - JUDICIAL RECOMMENDATION D - RELEASE RESIDENCE/PLANNING E - POPULATION MANAGEMENT	G - CIMS I - MED/PSYCH TREATMENT N - PROGRAM PARTICIPATION M - WORK CADRE	S - PSF WAIVED U - LONG TERM DETAINEE V - GREATER SECURITY W - LESSER SECURITY	
7. PUBLIC SAFETY FACTORS	A - NONE B - DISRUPTIVE GROUP (males only) C - GREATEST SEVERITY OFFENSE (males only) F - SEX OFFENDER G - THREAT TO GOVERNMENT OFFICIALS H - DEPORTABLE ALIEN		I - SENTENCE LENGTH (males only) K - VIOLENT BEHAVIOR (females only) L - SERIOUS ESCAPE M - PRISON DISTURBANCE N - JUVENILE VIOLENCE O - SERIOUS TELEPHONE ABUSE	

B. BASE SCORING

1. TYPE OF DETAINER	0 = NONE 1 = LOWEST/LOW MODERATE	3 = MODERATE 5 = HIGH	7 = GREATEST	
2. SEVERITY OF CURRENT OFFENSE	0 = LOWEST 1 = LOW MODERATE	3 = MODERATE 5 = HIGH	7 = GREATEST	
3. MONTHS TO RELEASE				
4. CRIMINAL HISTORY SCORE	0 = 0-1 2 = 2-3	4 = 4-6 6 = 7-9	8 = 10-12 10 = 13 +	

5. HISTORY OF ESCAPE OR ATTEMPTS		NONE	>15 YEARS	10-15 YEARS	5-10 YEARS	<5 YEARS
	MINOR	0	1	1	2	3
	SERIOUS	0	3(S)	3(S)	3(S)	3(S)

6. History of Violence		NONE	>15 YEARS	10-15 YEARS	5-10 YEARS	<5 YEARS
	MINOR	0	1	1	3	5
	SERIOUS	0	2	4	6	7

7. VOLUNTARY SURRENDER STATUS	0 = NOT APPLICABLE	(-3) = VOLUNTARY SURRENDER	
8. AGE	0 = 55 and over 2 = 36 through 54	4 = 25 through 35 8 = 24 or less	
9. EDUCATION LEVEL	0 = Verified High School Degree/GED 1 = Enrolled in and making satisfactory progress in GED Program 2 = No verified High School Degree/GED & not participating in GED Program		
10. DRUG/ALCOHOL ABUSE	0 = Never/>5 Years	1 = <5 Years	
11. BASE SCORE (ADD § B. ITEMS 1 - 10)			0

C. CUSTODY SCORING

1. PERCENTAGE OF TIME SERVED	3 = 0-25% 4 = 26-75%	5 = 76-90% 6 = 91+%		
2. PROGRAM PARTICIPATION	0 = POOR	1 = AVERAGE	2 = GOOD	
3. LIVING SKILLS	0 = POOR	1 = AVERAGE	2 = GOOD	
4. TYPE & NUMBER OF MOST SERIOUS INCIDENT RPT	0 = ANY GREAT (100) IN PAST 10 YRS 1 = > 1 HIGH (200) IN PAST 2 YRS 2(A) = 1 HIGH (200) IN PAST 2 YRS 2(B) = > 1 MOD (300) IN PAST YR	3(A) = 1 MOD (300) IN PAST YR 3(B) = >1 LOW MOD (400) IN PAST YR 4 = 1 LOW MOD (400) IN PAST YR 5 = NONE		
5. FREQUENCY OF INCIDENT REPORTS (IN PAST YEAR)	0 = 6+ 1 = 2 THRU 5	2 = ONE 3 = NONE		
6. FAMILY/COMMUNITY TIES	3 = NONE OR MINIMAL	4 = AVERAGE OR GOOD		
7. CUSTODY TOTAL (ADD § C. ITEMS 1 - 6)				0
8. CUSTODY VARIANCE (FROM APPROPRIATE TABLE ON TABLE CN BP-338, PAGE 2)				
9. SECURITY TOTAL (ADD OR SUBTRACT CUSTODY VARIANCE (§ C.8) TO BASE SCORE (§ B.11))				0
10. SCORED SECURITY LEVEL		11. MANAGEMENT SECURITY LEVEL		

HOW TO AVOID FEDERAL DRUG CONSPIRACY AND FIREARMS CHARGES

D. INSTITUTION ACTION

1. TYPE OF REVIEW: (EXCEPTION OR REGULAR)
2. CURRENT CUSTODY: (MAXIMUM, IN, OUT, COMMUNITY)
3. NEW CUSTODY: (MAXIMUM, IN, OUT, COMMUNITY)
4. ACTION: (APPROVE, DISAPPROVE)
5. DATE OF NEXT REVIEW
6. CHAIRPERSON

   NAME AND SIGNATURE

7. EXCEPTION REVIEW

   NAME (WARDEN OR DESIGNEE) AND SIGNATURE

8. SUMMARY OF FINAL ACTION   SECURITY LEVEL
                                  CUSTODY

CUSTODY CHANGE RECOMMENDATIONS BASED ON CUSTODY VARIANCE

IF CUSTODY VARIANCE IS IN THE (+) RANGE	CONSIDER A CUSTODY INCREASE
IF CUSTODY VARIANCE IS IN THE (-) RANGE	CONSIDER A CUSTODY DECREASE
IF CUSTODY VARIANCE IS ZERO	CONTINUE PRESENT CUSTODY

MALE CUSTODY VARIANCE TABLE — CUSTODY

SCORE		6	7	8	9	10	11	12	13	14	15	16	17	18	19	20	21	22
BASE	0-11	+4	+4	+3	+3	+2	+1	+1	+1	0	0	-1	-1	-2	-3	-4	-5	-5
SCORE	12-15	+4	+4	+3	+3	+2	+1	+1	+1	0	0	0	-1	-2	-3	-4	-5	-5
RANGE	16-23	+8	+6	+5	+4	+4	+3	+2	+1	+1	0	0	0	-1	-1	-2	-2	-3
	24+	+8	+6	+5	+4	+4	+3	+2	+1	+1	+1	0	0	0	-1	-1	-2	-3

FEMALE CUSTODY VARIANCE TABLE — CUSTODY

SCORE		6	7	8	9	10	11	12	13	14	15	16	17	18	19	20	21	22
BASE	0-15	+15	+11	+7	+4	+3	+2	+1	+1	0	0	0	0	-2	-4	-8	-12	-16
SCORE	16-30	+15	+11	+7	+4	+3	+2	+1	+1	0	0	0	0	0	-4	-8	-12	-16
RANGE	31+	+15	+11	+7	+4	+3	+2	+1	+1	0	0	0	0	0	0	-1	-5	-8

(This form may be replicated via WP)   Replaces BP-S338.051 of FEB 02

BP-338 page 2

DISCONTINUED PUBLIC SAFETY FACTORS
D   Firearms   E High Drug   J Designation Assessment

Table 5-2

SECURITY DESIGNATION TABLE (MALES)		
INMATE SECURITY LEVEL ASSIGNMENTS BASED ON CLASSIFICATION SCORE AND PUBLIC SAFETY FACTORS		
Security Point Total	Public Safety Factors	Inmate Security Level
0 - 11	**No Public Safety Factors**	**Minimum**
	Deportable Alien	Low
	Juvenile Violence	Low
	Greatest Severity Offense	Low
	Sex Offender	Low
	Serious Telephone Abuse	Low
	Threat to Government Officials	Low
	Sentence Length	
	Time remaining > 10 Yrs	Low
	Time remaining > 20 Yrs	Medium
	Time remaining > 30 Yrs (Includes non-parolable LIFE and Death penalty cases)	High
	Serious Escape	Medium
	Disruptive Group	High
	Prison Disturbance	High
12 - 15	**No Public Safety Factors**	**Low**
	Serious Escape	Medium
	Sentence Length	
	Time remaining > 20 Yrs	Medium
	Time remaining > 30 Yrs (Includes non-parolable LIFE and Death penalty cases)	High
	Disruptive Group	High
	Prison Disturbance	High
16 - 23	**No Public Safety Factors**	**Medium**
	Disruptive Group	High
	Prison Disturbance	High
	Sentence Length	
	Time remaining > 30 Yrs (Includes non-parolable LIFE and Death penalty cases)	High
24 +		**High**

Table 5-3

SECURITY DESIGNATION TABLE (FEMALES)		
INMATE SECURITY LEVEL ASSIGNMENTS BASED ON CLASSIFICATION SCORE AND PUBLIC SAFETY FACTORS		
Security Point Total	Public Safety Factors	Inmate Security Level
0 - 15	**No Public Safety Factors** Deportable Alien Juvenile Violence Serious Telephone Abuse Sex Offender Threat to Government Officials Violent Behavior Prison Disturbance Serious Escape	**Minimum** Low Low Low Low Low Low High High
16 - 30	**No Public Safety Factors** Prison Disturbance Serious Escape	**Low** High High
31 +		**High**

PRISONS

USP Pollock (adjacent satellite camp)

FCI Ray Brook

FMC Rochester

FCI Safford

MCC San Diego

FCI Sandstone

FCI Schuylkill (adjacent satellite camp)

FCI Seagoville (adjacent satellite camp)

FDC Sea Tac

FCI Sheridan (adjacent satellite camp)

MCFP Springfield

TCI Taft (adjacent satellite camp)

FCI Talladega (adjacent satellite camp)

FCI Tallahassee

FCI Terminal Island

FCI Terre Haute

USP Terre Haute (adjacent satellite camp)

FCI Texarkana (adjacent satellite camp)

FCI Three Rivers (adjacent satellite camp) FCI Tucson

FCI Victorville - Medium I (adjacent satellite camp)

FCI Victorville - Medium II

USP Victorville

HOW TO AVOID FEDERAL DRUG CONSPIRACY AND FIREARMS CHARGES

FCI Waseca

FPC Yankton

FCI Yazoo City - Low (adjacent satellite camp)

FCI Yazoo City - Medium

FCI Fort Dix (adjacent satellite camp)

FMC Fort Worth

FCI Gilmer (adjacent satellite camp)

FCI Greenville (adjacent satellite camp)

MDC Guaynabo

USP Hazelton (adjacent satellite camp)

FCI Herlong (adjacent satellite camp)

FDC Honolulu

FDC Houston

FCI Jesup (adjacent satellite camp)

FCI La Tuna (adjacent satellite camp)

USP Leavenworth (adjacent satellite camp)

USP Lee (adjacent satellite camp)

USP Lewisburg (adjacent satellite camp)

FMC Lexington (adjacent satellite camp)

FCI Lompoc

USP Lompoc (adjacent satellite camp)

FCI Loretto (adjacent satellite camp)

MDC Los Angeles

FCI Manchester (adjacent satellite camp)

FCI Marianna (adjacent satellite camp)

USP Marion (adjacent satellite camp)

USP McCreary

FCI McKean (adjacent satellite camp)

FCI Memphis (adjacent satellite camp)

FCI Miami (adjacent satellite camp)

FDC Miami

FCI Milan

FPC Montgomery

FCI Morgantown

MCC New York

FCI Oakdale

FDC Oakdale (adjacent satellite camp)

FTC Oklahoma City

FCI Otisville (adjacent satellite camp)

FCI Oxford (adjacent satellite camp)

FPC Pensacola

FCI Pekin

FCI Petersburg - Low (adjacent satellite camp)

FCI Petersburg - Medium

FDC Philadelphia

FCI Phoenix (adjacent satellite camp)

FPC Alderson

FCI Allenwood - Low

FCI Allenwood - Medium

USP Allenwood

FCI Ashland (adjacent satellite camp)

USP Atlanta (adjacent satellite camp)

USP Atwater

FCI Bastrop (adjacent satellite camp)

FCI Beaumont - Low

FCI Beaumont - Medium

USP Beaumont (adjacent satellite camp)

FCI Beckley (adjacent satellite camp)

USP Big Sandy (adjacent satellite camp)

FCI Big Spring (adjacent satellite camp)

MDC Brooklyn

FPC Bryan

FCI Butner - Low

FCI Butner - Medium (adjacent satellite camp)

FMC Butner

USP Canaan (adjacent satellite camp)

FMC Carswell

MCC Chicago

FCI Coleman - Low

FCI Coleman - Medium (adjacent satellite camp)

USP Coleman I

USP Coleman II

FCI Cumberland (adjacent satellite camp)

FCI Danbury (adjacent satellite camp)

FMC Devens (adjacent satellite camp)

FCI Dublin (adjacent satellite camp)

FPC Duluth

FCI Edgefield (adjacent satellite camp)

FCI El Reno (adjacent satellite camp)

FCI Elkton - Low (adjacent satellite camp)

FCI Englewood (adjacent satellite camp)

FCI Estill (adjacent satellite camp)

FCI Fairton (adjacent satellite camp)

FCI Florence (adjacent satellite camp)

USP Florence ADMAX

USP Florence - High

FCI Forrest City - Low (adjacent satellite low)

FCI Forrest City - Medium

Federal Correctional Institution, Safford - Safford, Arizona

Federal Correctional Institution, Sandstone - Sandstone, Minnesota

Federal Correctional Institution, Schuylkill - Minersville, Pennsylvania

Federal Correctional Institution, Seagoville - Seagoville, Texas

HOW TO AVOID FEDERAL DRUG CONSPIRACY AND FIREARMS CHARGES

Federal Correctional Institution, Sheridan - Sheridan, Oregon

Federal Correctional Institution, Talladega - Talladega, Alabama

Federal Correctional Institution, Tallahassee - Tallahassee, Florida

Federal Correctional Institution, Terminal Island - Terminal Island, California

Federal Correctional Institution, Texarkana - Texarkana, Texas

Federal Correctional Institution, Three Rivers - Three Rivers, Texas

Federal Correctional Institution, Tucson - Tucson, Arizona

Federal Correctional Institution, Victorville - Adelanto, California

Federal Correctional Institution, Waseca - Waseca, Minnesota

Federal Correctional Institution, Williamsburg - Salters, South Carolina

Federal Correctional Institution, Yazoo City - Yazoo City, Mississippi

Federal Detention Center, Honolulu - Honolulu, Hawaii

Federal Detention Center, Houston - Houston, Texas

Federal Detention Center, Miami - Miami, Florida

Federal Detention Center, Oakdale - Oakdale, Louisiana

Federal Detention Center, Philadelphia - Philadelphia, Pennsylvania

Federal Detention Center, SeaTac - Seattle, Washington

Federal Medical Center, Carswell - Fort Worth, Texas

Federal Medical Center, Devens - Devens, Massachusetts

Federal Medical Center, Fort Worth - Fort Worth, Texas

Federal Medical Center, Lexington - Lexington, Kentucky

Federal Medical Center, Rochester - Rochester, Minnesota

Federal Prison Camp, Alderson Alderson, West Virginia

Federal Prison Camp, Allenwood - Montgomery, Pennsylvania

Federal Prison Camp, Bryan - Bryan, Texas

Federal Prison Camp, Devens - Devens, Massachusetts

Federal Prison Camp, Duluth - Duluth, Minnesota

Federal Prison Camp, Eglin - Eglin Air Force Base, Florida

Federal Prison Camp, Leavenworth - Leavenworth, Kansas

Federal Prison Camp, Montgomery - Montgomery, Alabama

Federal Prison Camp, Nellis - North Las Vegas, Nevada

Federal Prison Camp, Pensacola - Pensacola, Florida

Federal Prison Camp, Seymour Johnson - Goldsboro, North Carolina

Federal Prison Camp, Yankton - Yankton, South Dakota

Federal Secure Low La Tuna - El Paso, Texas

Federal Transfer Center, Oklahoma City - Oklahoma City, Oklahoma

United States Medical Center for Federal Prisoners - Springfield, Missouri

Metropolitan Correctional Center, Chicago - Chicago, Illinois

Metropolitan Correctional Center, New York - New York, New York

Metropolitan Correctional Center, San Diego - San Diego, California

Metropolitan Detention Center, Brooklyn - Brooklyn, New York

Metropolitan Detention Center, Guaynabo - Guaynabo, Puerto Rico

Metropolitan Detention Center, Los Angeles - Los Angeles, California

United States Penitentiary, Allenwood - Montgomery, Pennsylvania

United States Penitentiary, Atlanta - Atlanta, Georgia

United States Penitentiary, Atwater - Atwater, California

United States Penitentiary, Beaumont - Beaumont, Texas

United States Penitentiary, Big Sandy - Inez, Kentucky

United States Penitentiary, Florence - Florence, Colorado

United States Penitentiary, Leavenworth - Leavenworth, Kansas

United States Penitentiary, Lee - Jonesville, Virginia

United States Penitentiary, Lewisburg - Lewisburg, Pennsylvania

United States Penitentiary, Lompoc - Lompoc, California

United States Penitentiary, Marion - Marion, Illinois

United States Penitentiary, McCreary - McCreary County, Kentucky

United States Penitentiary, Pollock - Pollock, Louisiana

United States Penitentiary, Terre Haute - Terre Haute, Indiana

United States Penitentiary, Victorville - Victorville, California

References

"Weekly Population Report". Bureau of Prisons. http://bop.gov/locations/weekly_report.jsp

Retrieved on 2009-01-22. Retrieved from
http://en.wikipedia.org/wiki/List_of_U.S._federal_prisons

The total population is 201,518 inmates. [1]

Federal Correctional Complex, Beaumont - Beaumont, Texas

Federal Correctional Complex, Butner - Butner, North Carolina

Federal Correctional Complex, Coleman - Coleman, Florida

Federal Correctional Complex, Petersburg - Petersburg, Virginia

Federal Correctional Complex, Terre Haute - Terre Haute, Indiana

Federal Correctional Institution, Allenwood - Montgomery, Pennsylvania

Federal Correctional Institution, Ashland - Ashland, Kentucky

Federal Correctional Institution, Bastrop - Bastrop, Texas

Federal Correctional Institution, Beaumont - Beaumont, Texas

Federal Correctional Institution, Beckley - Beaver, West Virginia

Federal Correctional Institution, Bennettsville - Bennettsville, South Carolina

Federal Correctional Institution, Big Spring - Big Spring, Texas

Federal Correctional Institution, Butner - Butner, North Carolina

Federal Correctional Institution, Coleman - Coleman, Florida

Federal Correctional Institution, Cumberland - Cumberland, Maryland

Federal Correctional Institution, Danbury - Danbury, Connecticut

Federal Correctional Institution, Dublin - Dublin, California

Federal Correctional Institution, Edgefield - Edgefield, South Carolina

Federal Correctional Institution, El Reno - El Reno, Oklahoma

Federal Correctional Institution, Elkton - Elkton, Ohio

Federal Correctional Institution, Englewood - Lakewood, Colorado

Federal Correctional Institution, Estill - Estill, South Carolina

Federal Correctional Institution, Fairton - Fairton, New Jersey

Federal Correctional Institution, Florence - Florence, Colorado

Federal Correctional Complex, Forrest City - Forrest City, Arkansas

Federal Correctional Institution, Fort Dix - Fort Dix, New Jersey

Federal Correctional Institution, Fort Worth - Fort Worth, Texas

Federal Correctional Institution, Gilmer - Glenville, West Virginia

Federal Correctional Institution, Greenville - Greenville, Illinois

Federal Correctional Institution, Herlong - Herlong, California

Federal Correctional Institution, Jesup - Jesup, Georgia

Federal Correctional Institution, La Tuna - Anthony, Texas

Federal Correctional Institution, Lompoc - Lompoc, California

Federal Correctional Institution, Loretto - Loretto, Pennsylvania

Federal Correctional Institution, Manchester - Manchester, Kentucky

Federal Correctional Institution, Marianna - Marianna, Florida

Federal Correctional Institution, McKean - Bradford, Pennsylvania

Federal Correctional Institution, Memphis - Memphis, Tennessee

Federal Correctional Institution, Mendota - Mendota, California

Federal Correctional Institution, Miami - Miami, Florida

Federal Correctional Institution, Milan - Milan, Michigan

Federal Correctional Institution, Morgantown - Morgantown, West Virginia

Federal Correctional Institution, Oakdale - Oakdale, Louisiana

Federal Correctional Institution, Otisville - Otisville, New York

Federal Correctional Institution, Oxford - Oxford, Wisconsin

Federal Correctional Institution, Pekin - Pekin, Illinois

Federal Correctional Institution, Phoenix - Phoenix, Arizona

Federal Correctional Institution, Ray Brook - North Elba, New York

HOW TO AVOID FEDERAL DRUG CONSPIRACY AND FIREARMS CHARGES

Made in United States
Orlando, FL
11 April 2022

16746563R00055